C000068366

Exchanging the truth of God for a lie
(Romans 1:25)

One man's spiritual journey to find the truth
about homosexuality and same-sex partnerships

by Jeremy Marks

Foreword by Roy Clements

*This book is dedicated to all lesbian & gay people everywhere who
have struggled to understand the truth of God about homosexuality
and find reconciliation between their faith and sexuality.*

First published in 2008 by Courage UK
www.courage.org.uk

Printed by RPM, Chichester
Print production by RoperPenberthy Publishing Ltd
PO Box 545, Horsham, RH12 4QW

ISBN 978-1-903905-34-0

What people are saying about this book

"There is a kind of strength, an ability to stand up and tell the truth, to be penitent about what must be repented of and bold about what must be affirmed, that is not a matter of having worked something out, having a fine intellect or an elegant style. It is a matter of having been taken through the wringer, brought to the end of oneself and re-built by the Spirit from the foundations up. This is the kind of strength that was promised to Peter after he had been "sifted like wheat" so that he could turn and confirm his brethren. You know it when you see it, and I see it here, in Jeremy's narrative. You can of course ignore it, but should you choose to read it you will find it very difficult to drive anything at all between this testimony of a true Pastor and the Rock on which that testimony is founded."

James Alison, Catholic theologian, priest and author

"Jeremy Marks has witnessed at first hand through 20 years of working with lesbian and gay Christians the blessings given to them by God and brought by them to the church. He has also witnessed the failure of programmes to change or suppress a person's sexual identity and the spiritual, financial, mental and emotional devastation these programmes can cause.

Jeremy's account is rooted in scripture, in profound self-examination and a radical, fearless openness to God and to the truth of his experience. Jeremy has lived his own journey to self-acceptance as a gay man. No-one reading this book can doubt the integrity of his own faith and the witness to God's creative love at work in the lives of lesbian and gay Christians and of the Spirit of God at work in the church, challenging prejudice and all that denies our full humanity in Christ.

Will those who need to read this book have the courage to engage with its implications and follow Jeremy's testimony through to the radical conclusions reached by Courage? I hope and pray they will."

Colin Coward, Director of Changing Attitude, England

"Jeremy's story shines with courage, pastoral experience, spiritual reflection and a passion for seeking truth and sharing Christ with the hurt and lost. However, many evangelicals will find this book challenging and uncomfortable because we cannot fully agree with where Jeremy's pilgrimage has taken him. The temptation will be to ignore or dismiss his testimony but if we really care about developing a Christ-like response to gay and lesbian people we need to read it and seek alternative answers to the questions it raises." Andrew Goddard

ii

"This book is timely and important. The consequences of the ex-gay movement are little known and little understood. Jeremy Marks' wisdom and faith mean that he can give an honest account of the assumptions and actions of the movement. He shows how a healthy view of human sexuality can lead into deeper faith in Jesus Christ. I commend it."

Giles Goddard, Inclusive Church

"Throughout its ministry Courage has ministered the Gospel to gay people with love, compassion and integrity. This timely and honest account of its history will show anyone who is open to both the love of Christ and the authority of Scripture, how it is possible for Evangelicals to become 'gay-affirming' and yet stay true to the Christian faith as they have received it. In changing its approach to gay & lesbian people, 'Courage' has been true to its name and showed leadership that is both rare and remarkable in following Jesus Christ, The Way, The Truth, and The Life. We should all be challenged and inspired by their example."

Rev Benny Hazlehurst, founder of Accepting Evangelicals

"This brave book tells the inside story about 'ex gay' ministries, and exposes the secret pathologies that often lie behind religious hostility to same-sex relationships. It should be required reading for Christian leaders and anyone else who is concerned about the Church's attitude to gay people."

Jeffrey John, Dean of St Albans

"As he unfolds the conflict between his own faith and sexuality, with warmth and wisdom, Jeremy Marks reveals the struggles of countless people who, in spite of the homophobia and the fear-induced theology that has paralysed much of the Church, have chosen courageously to walk with integrity as Christians – who also happen to be gay, lesbian, bisexual or transgender. As one who survived 17 years myself – suppressing my gay orientation and trying to change – Jeremy's book will help ex-gay survivors and those who love them to understand better what we did to ourselves (what we let others do to us) and why."

Peterson Toscano, co-founder of www.BeyondExGay.com

Further material by Jeremy Marks
and an archive of articles and sermons written by Dr Roy Clements
can be found at www.courage.org.uk

N.B. *Courage UK is not the Catholic ministry promoting chastity founded by Father John Harvey (based in New York, with other branches worldwide). Details about that organisation, may be found at www.couragerc.org. The UK branch of CourageRC (known as EnCourage) can be found at www.encouragetrust.org.uk.*

Acknowledgements

I have been indebted to so many wonderful men and women throughout my life and spiritual journey. To give them credit here would make a very long list. Unfortunately, given the highly contentious subject matter of this book, many of them would probably not thank me for mentioning them. And if I were only to mention those who do not mind, it would look very odd to leave out those who do. They know who they are. They also know, I am sure, how grateful I am to them for their love and support over many years, especially since starting the *Courage* ministry in 1988.

Someone I *can* mention here is Brian Longman, who has helped me in the *Courage* office in a voluntary capacity since 2002; he could not have been a more faithful helper and co-worker. I will also mention Roy Clements who has kindly written the foreword and whose support and friendship I have come to appreciate so much. Angie Moyler has designed the cover and her husband Tim Moyler, a long-standing friend, advised on printing and publication. I am indebted also to David Page who, at very short notice, revised and edited the whole text, endeavouring to turn my somewhat meandering and wordy original manuscript into something more readable!

Above all my wife Bren has courageously and faithfully stuck with me on a turbulent and traumatic path, as we've journeyed from our beginnings as a conservative evangelical ministry — when we called for gay Christians to struggle with and *overcome* their homosexuality — to a place of acceptance and affirmation of gay people and same-sex relationships. Few wives would have stuck so steadfastly through the challenges, with levels of psychological pain that would test most marriages to extinction. Though our relationship did not begin as a romance in the most conventional heterosexual way, our love and support for one another has withstood extraordinary levels of testing and been strengthened immeasurably, since we married in 1991.

A popular myth among 'ex-gay' ministries, such as we once were, is that homosexuality comes about as the result of poor parenting. I therefore want to take this opportunity to give thanks to God especially for my wonderful parents. I don't believe I could possibly have had a more wonderful Mum and Dad than mine. I am so grateful for their love, friendship and support. I am also blessed with two fabulous sisters who are true saints. Jesus would surely say of my wife and family that they are *the salt of the earth.* (Matthew 5:13). I love them all very dearly.   Jeremy Marks

Contents

About the author

Born in London, UK in 1952, Jeremy Marks was the oldest of three children, and brought up in the Anglican Church, a tradition he rejected for a time after witnessing the hostility and hypocrisy suffered by his parents around the time of their divorce in 1968. Having begun to realise he was gay by the age of 13, it soon became obvious that the Church would be hostile to homosexual people too. However, he found his faith again at the age of 21 thanks to the witness of a school friend, and was baptised as a believer.

He spent the next seven years at Guildford Baptist Church enjoying the exceptional expository Bible teaching ministry of the Revd J. David Pawson. Lacking experience of any tradition other than the CofE, he was unaware how very traditional an evangelical foundation this church had, in effect anti-gay by doctrinal conviction (though not actually hostile to those whose 'behaviour was under control'). One of the great attractions of this church was perhaps the sense of security in belonging to a Christian fellowship where first class Bible teaching, preaching of the Gospel and commitment to the truth (certainty) was paramount. In an environment where coming to terms with being gay was anathema, paradoxically it was quite affirming to be counted among those who were prepared to 'crucify their sinful nature' for Christ's sake – making a virtue of internalised homophobia!

After three years vocational training at art college before taking up a career in professional architectural photography, Jeremy worked for 11 years for a publishing company, that involved country-wide travel and necessitated moving to Watford. He joined the charismatic House Church Movement (part of New Frontiers International), where it seemed that healing of homosexuality was to be expected because 'nothing is impossible for God'. However, after many years of receiving counselling, deliverance, healing prayer and even secular psychotherapy, Jeremy found no relief from his acute sense of loneliness or from being plagued by internal conflict over his sexuality. He then discovered the 'ex-gay' movement in 1986. Although really just offering more of the same kind of approach, the ex-gay movement did open up the possibility of travelling with other gay Christian strugglers, which was a significant step forwards – helping to assuage the acute sense of isolation and loneliness.

In 1987, an opportunity arose to visit *Love in Action* in San Raphael California, founded by Frank Worthen, a ministry that was part of a Community Church known as the "Church of the Open Door". The *Love in Action* discipleship houses at that time offered tremendous support for those gay Christians who were committed to the ex-gay process. This seemed such a radical, exciting, cutting-edge ministry, also built on a reassuringly solid biblical basis, that Jeremy gave up his career in photography and spent four months working with this ministry on a training basis.

In February 1988, after Jeremy had returned home, he founded *Courage* (UK) under the auspices of his local church – the New Life Church Harrow – and *Courage* became one of the leading Christian ministries in the UK for lesbian & gay Christians committed to the ex-gay ideal. With a dedicated team of co-workers, *Courage* began offering the "Steps out of Homosexuality" discipleship course by Frank Worthen on a residential basis as from 1989.

In 1991, he married his wife Bren, who also took a keen interest in the work. However, at the end of 1994, for various practical and financial reasons, the live-houses had to be closed down; weekly discipleship group meetings provided the vehicle for ongoing pastoral care. During the rest of the 1990's, Jeremy became increasingly concerned at the lack of good fruit from this form of ministry over the long term. It gradually became more and more obvious that the ex-gay process did not work and that the people who were doing well were those who accepted they were gay and found a same-sex partnership. During this period, Jeremy served on the board of *Exodus International Europe*, a coalition of ex-gay ministries.

vii

Twelve years after *Courage* was founded, at the end of 2000, Jeremy startled the evangelical world by publicly repudiating the ex-gay movement, proclaiming that it did more harm than good. *Courage* then embraced an unequivocally gay-affirming approach, recognising the despair that had resulted for so many sincere Christian folk who had tried the 'ex-gay' approach. Unsurprisingly this resulted in expulsion from *Exodus International*, the *Evangelical Alliance* and rejection from other evangelical Christian groups with whom he had been involved for many years. Their action was, however, counted a blessing by Jeremy, who then felt released to speak more candidly about his experience and new-found conviction. He was also immensely grateful for a new source of moral support from Dr Ralph Blair, founder of *Evangelicals Concerned* (www.ecinc.org and www.ecwr.org); Dr Blair's many years of experience supporting openly gay Christians had clearly borne good fruit that has lasted, proving the efficacy of a gay-affirming Christian message.

Since the turn of the Millenium, *Courage* has continued to offer pastoral care and support to a great many gay Christians, coming mainly from evangelical backgrounds. Having felt destroyed by their Churches, these gay Christians are in the process of recovering their self-esteem and learning to accept their homosexuality as a gift from God.

Jeremy Marks, June 2008

For further information about the work of *Courage*, please go to:

www.courage.org.uk

Or you can write to Jeremy Marks at the *Courage* office:

COURAGE
PO Box 748
GUILDFORD
GU1 2ZY
United Kingdom

E-mail: office@courage.org.uk

Foreword

A pilgrim is one who makes of their journey an act of worship and spiritual discovery. This is the story of such a pilgrimage. Not a crusade, you understand. Our pilgrim did not entertain any ambition to win honour for himself as a warrior for the Christian cause nor did he seek to extend the powerbase of any Christian church or organisation. No, the only battles he wanted to fight were within himself. For this pilgrim, you see, was gay.

At the outset, he would have refused to accept that label, believing that homosexuality was a choice not an identity, a sinful practice not an innate orientation. Indeed, when the pilgrimage began, the destination he sought was a place of deliverance from all such homosexual temptations. As his journey proceeded, however, that goal grew ever more elusive. Eventually he came to the disturbing conclusion that it was in fact a mirage — a specious illusion that was deceitfully drawing him, not to a life-giving oasis, but deeper and deeper into a spiritual desert. He was gay, and no amount of prayer and spiritual discipline would ever make him truly 'ex-gay'.

Some pilgrims at this point would have abandoned the journey. Perhaps, like Cain, homosexuals are branded as irredeemable exiles by their crime. Perhaps, like Esau, they can find no place of repentance even though they seek it with tears. But our pilgrim refused to yield to such apostasy. In the slough of despond, where cynicism, despair and hate could so easily have claimed him, he clung on to faith, hope and love. They led him to a turning point, a new direction and a far more satisfactory destination.

This book, as I say, is the story of that journey. It is not a systematic or logical account, because the journey did not happen that way. Many things had an influence on our pilgrim as he pursued his meandering and often uncertain itinerary: reflection on biblical texts; encounters with fellow-travellers; life experiences, both positive and negative; and, most significant of all, moments of fresh insight given, he is convinced, by the Spirit of Christ. He has laid them all out for us, like a scattered collage of diary entries. Those who come looking for a rigorous theological apologia will be disappointed therefore. But those who genuinely want to understand the struggles of a gay Christian will find this spiritual travelogue full of interest. The author does not pretend to have all the answers, but through times of considerable personal pain and sacrifice, in my judgement at least, he has proven himself to be a wise pastor, an honest man and a worthy Christian pilgrim.

Roy Clements, London, 2008

Author's Note on Romans 1:25

It is this author's conviction that there is no such thing as *the truth of God* as distinct from any other kind of 'truth' that is not of God. From a Christian point of view, a belief or doctrine claiming to be another kind of truth in opposition to the truth of God is what we call *falsehood*. It also follows that when we discover something to be true, then we have discovered something that is of God, because God is Truth. In fact the truth informs us about God. As Paul writes, in Romans 1:19,20 . . . *since what may be known about God is plain to them, because God has made it plain to them. For since the creation of the world God's invisible qualities – his eternal power and divine nature – have been clearly seen, being understood from what has been made, so that men are without excuse.* So according to scriptures, in the first instance, from Creation, clearly God did not begin by giving man a book about himself, for us to learn from.

When Paul writes about those who *exchanged the truth of God for a lie*, his sentence is completed with the words, *and worshipped and served created things rather than the Creator – who is forever praised. Amen.* Exchanging the truth of God for a lie is therefore is about wilfully changing our focus from God our Creator to the pursue the sinful agenda of man; as Paul puts it (vs 23) *exchanging the glory of the immortal God for images . . .* Given that our understanding of God today, as Christians, may well begin with the study of the scriptures and then become informed to a greater degree by our experience of life, the difference between truth and falsehood is not always as obvious as it may seem – especially to people of religious conviction.

This book is the story of a journey to discover the truth of God about homosexuality and the acceptability of same-sex partnerships. The journey continues . . .

© Jeremy Marks, 2008

The right of Jeremy Marks to be identified as the Author of this work has been asserted in accordance with the Copyright, Designs and Patents Act 1998.

Exchanging the truth of God for a lie

(Romans 1:25 NIV)

1. The Healing Power of Love

Early in the 1990s I received a telephone call from a pastor asking if *Courage* could help a member of his congregation who, it had emerged, was gay. This pastor regarded the matter as so urgent that he was prepared to undertake a three hundred mile round trip to bring this church member to Watford where our residential discipleship houses were based. It turned out that the man he wanted to bring — I'll call him Robert — had been through a series of disastrous situations which were so emotionally shattering that he had ended up making a very serious suicide attempt. Underlying these events, which would have been devastating for anybody, lay a deep inner conflict because of his homosexuality. The pastor felt out of his depth and, it seemed to me that the thought of being able to send Robert to a residential course to resolve this was so appealing to him that, if he could have just put him on a train with a one-way ticket, it would have been ideal. But we never took anyone who had simply been sent. People only came because, after careful consideration, they freely chose to do so.

From the outset, we made it clear that we were not qualified to deal with the underlying emotional and psychological issues that Robert was struggling with. All we could offer was a welcome into a caring community. Hopefully, that would give him some respite from the awful catalogue of disasters he had been through, and help him recover. We all need a caring community around us at times, to help us through a difficult period in our lives. But we knew that ultimately nobody changes unless they really want to. We endeavoured to be God's family and cared deeply for everyone who came.

On the basis of his initial visit, Robert decided he would like to come, and he joined us within a few weeks. Our *Steps Out of Homosexuality* programme was not due to restart until the New Year so, for the first three months, he just enjoyed a relaxing time with us to recover. In fact he turned out to be a tremendous answer to our prayers. The *Courage* computer had crashed and we had lost our entire database. When we tried to access the backup disks, we discovered they had become corrupted and were useless. So we had been praying for someone who could come and rebuild the database. This was a task that suited Robert down to the ground as he was very skilled in this area. It was a therapeutic job for him as well as being an answer to our prayers. Robert really enjoyed those first three months.

When he began the discipleship programme, however, problems began. Robert was a brilliantly clever man with many years experience of life behind him. He had run big businesses and projects that would have been far beyond me. He always believed he knew better than we did how to run the ministry and never lost an opportunity to try and put us right. Sometimes he did this with a wry and witty sense of humour but at other times with plain vitriol. At the end of that year, though I knew in my heart that God wanted him to stay on and I have always believed in the importance of trusting and obeying God, I had reached my limits. I could not wait for the year to end and for him to leave. I was not easily going to be persuaded otherwise. Then, to my astonishment and entirely unprompted by me, Robert came into my office and admitted he had given us a terrible time, declaring how sorry he was. He said that although he really wanted to leave, he knew God wanted him to stay. Since we were agreed on that, I relented. He became a little more contrite and things got better for a while. But after another six months, we all recognised that the time really had come for him to move on. We parted on a friendly basis, believing that God must have accomplished whatever it was he wanted to do in Robert's life at that point. He returned to his home town.

We kept in touch for some time after that but gradually, as so often happens in life, we saw less and less of him. About five years later, we learned to our horror, that Robert had once again made a massive suicide attempt. He had really intended to succeed and was none too pleased to wake up in intensive care and find he was still in this world. The circumstances in which he was discovered and rushed to hospital were, to my mind, quite miraculous. Robert may not have wanted to stay on this earth any longer, but clearly God had decided that his time had not yet come. The doctors told him that he had overdosed so seriously that he would never be fit enough to work again. While he was convalescing, I visited him as often as I could, to offer support and also because I wanted to understand the reasons for him being so severely traumatised.

We had now reached the early years of the internet and e-mail. Robert was still an expert computer buff and had little else to do with his time other than spend it on the computer. Some time later he phoned me, absolutely jubilant, to tell me that he had met someone on-line and fallen in love. In view of Robert's vehemently expressed conviction in the past that homosexuality was a poison of diabolical inspiration, I was rather surprised to discover that the love of his life was a man. Within a few months, this relationship had blossomed and he rang again to say he was moving to another part of the country where they would live together. I lost touch with him for almost ten years. When I wanted to ask his permission to use his story in this book, it took me some time to track Robert down. He is still living with the man he fell in love with and they are in business together, doing very well. Within a year of their meeting, Robert's health had recovered, defying the prognosis of the doctors.

Robert's story is one of any number I could tell. It powerfully demonstrates that when people come to terms with who they are and are able to enjoy a committed relationship of mutual love, profound healing can happen which is far more effective than any ministry process I know of.

I had always hoped that *Courage* would achieve this kind of outcome, but in heterosexual terms. Yet, by finding love in a gay relationship, not only had Robert discovered the healing he so needed, but he was also now able to enjoy life and live it to the full. His experience brought healing to our relationship too. When people are at war with themselves, it is not unusual for them to be at war with everyone else as well. They can certainly be very difficult to live with. At the lowest point in his life Robert had discovered the bankruptcy of all his and our strategies for godly living as we then understood it. He had realised that God loved him unconditionally and accepted him just as he was — as a gay man. Only then had he found the gateway to healing and wholeness.

There is no more powerful a challenge to your assumptions than witnessing a real event where the outcome defies your expectations. Jesus demonstrated the authority of his calling again and again through miracles of healing which helped persuade his followers to listen to him, to realise who he was, to face up to the huge challenges his message posed and to be transformed. Some of Jesus' followers ended up being willing to die for him, others wanted to kill him. Truth sometimes has this tendency to divide rather than unite. Here's Eugene Peterson's rendering of that striking passage in John 10 where people struggled to respond to what they had seen:

Jesus said, "I'm only quoting your inspired Scriptures, where God said, 'I tell you — you are gods.' If God called your ancestors 'gods' — and Scripture doesn't lie — why do you yell, 'Blasphemer! Blasphemer!' at the unique One the Father consecrated and sent into the world, just because I said, 'I am the Son of God'? If I don't do the things my Father does, well and good; don't believe me. But if I am doing them, put aside for a moment what you hear me say about myself and just take the evidence of the actions that are right before your eyes. Then perhaps things will come together for you, and you'll see that not only are we doing the same thing, we are the same – Father and Son. He is in me; I am in him." (John 10:34-38 The Message)

2.   The Depth of Submission

This book is the story of how the work I started – a traditional evangelical Christian ministry called *Courage* – changed its whole approach to the pastoral care of lesbian, gay and bisexual Christians.[1] It is much more than a change of approach, though. It is the story of a group of Christians who came to realise that God calls us to more than repentance and more than dutiful obedience to a set of rules. As we follow Christ, God calls us to become imitators of the one we worship (Ephesians 5:1-2). This calling will mean transformation at every level. And those who embark on this pilgrimage have Good News to share – the greatest imaginable news and the greatest possible cause for rejoicing – for the whole of mankind.

Courage was founded in February 1988 under the auspices of my local church.[2] The ministry was set up to support gay Christian people (like myself) who found themselves alone and disenfranchised by their churches. Having struggled with same-sex attractions for over twenty years, I knew there was very little help available. There was even less on offer in the way of hope.

We were all conservative evangelical Christians who shared the view that the union of a man and a woman fulfils God's purposes for mankind. Marriage and family life were the essential building blocks for a stable society. We believed that homosexual orientation was contrary to God's creation and that the practice of homosexuality was sinful. We took the popularly caricatured spread of gay lifestyles as indicative of the moral collapse of our society.

Our emphasis was always on developing a relationship with Christ above all, and on supporting one another on our Christian pilgrimage. If homosexuality was a sign of rebellion against God (Romans 1:18-32), then restoration of our relationship with God would be the remedy for sexual deviancy.

We began by offering pastoral care through weekly support groups for evangelical Christians who were struggling with homosexuality. Within a year we were also able to offer a year-long residential course called *Steps Out Of Homosexuality*. This excellent discipleship programme had been developed by Frank Worthen of Love in Action[3], an *Exodus* ministry based in San Rafael, California. *Exodus* is a coalition of 'ex-gay' ministries. I had trained with Frank and his wife Anita at *Love in Action* in 1987. Frank generously allowed us to use his programme because he wanted to see a similar ministry develop in the UK. The programme would have been good for any Christian. The content was centred on knowing Christ, not around homosexuality, and every aspect of it offered good basic teaching for anyone who wanted to follow Christ.

Our aim in the first instance was to encourage and support people to live a celibate life. Our guiding ethos could be summarised in a dictum of Oswald Chambers: *The depth of submission equals the height of victory.* The remedy for anyone who fell sexually was to repent and submit their life to God once again. This they would do as often as necessary. Unfortunately, this strategy meant there was never any possibility of us re-evaluating our understanding of human nature from the viewpoint of the God of all grace. Nor was there any possibility of re-examining any aspect of biblical teaching. We all believed that certain truths were fixed by God for all time and non-negotiable. This way of looking at scripture was the hallmark of all the evangelical Christians I knew. Many of us found a great sense of security in this approach. It never occurred to us that our reading of scripture was profoundly coloured by our own cultural context and world view. We accused liberals of picking and choosing from scripture, and did not see that we were doing the same thing ourselves. We failed altogether to realise that we were mistaking our limited perceptions for incontrovertible facts.

We also sought to go further than repentance. We looked for a way out of a homosexual orientation, believing that a life of Christian discipleship in a supportive fellowship which offered healing prayer could make this possible. Our involvement in the charismatic movement helped foster this hope of healing. We were also influenced by Andy Comiskey, founder of *Desert Stream Ministries* and author of the *Living Waters* programme; Mario Bergner, of *Redeemed Lives Ministry* and author of *Setting Love in Order*; and Leanne Payne of *Pastoral Care Ministries*, author of *The Broken Image* and many other books.

3.   An Intoxicating Fantasy

There can be no doubt that the charismatic movement made a very positive impact on evangelical churches, revitalising the faith of many Christians. Moreover, it released many ordinary people to contribute their gifts to the life of the church, rather than focusing everything on a trained pastorate. There was a new sense in which everybody belonged and everybody counted. Before long, we were all motivated by the expectation of revival. We believed we would see an outpouring of the Holy Spirit as in New Testament times, with miracles and the power of God manifested in astounding ways. This would herald the return of Jesus and the end of this Age. None of us wanted to miss out on a revival we felt sure would come — provided we had faith and thoroughly prepared ourselves for it. In the grand scheme of things, overcoming homosexuality was surely a trifling matter for a God for whom *nothing is impossible* (Matthew 19:26).

From the moment I began the ministry of *Courage* with a small team of the most dedicated co-workers anyone could wish for, we faced one enormous hurdle after another. Yet our faith and optimism was such, we believed that if we were in the will of God, we just could not fail, however great the challenges. After all, the Bible promised that the Christian life would mean hardship — so challenges were sent by God to be overcome, and we were not to allow them to defeat us.

As I saw it, the Christian life was to be one of chastity and obedience. I was not so sure about poverty — abstemiousness yes — but I saw poverty as something shameful. God's gracious provision of everything we legitimately needed was a promise we just had to believe in (Luke 12:22-34). Moreover we believed God would provide everything with a generosity of spirit, as certainly as we believed he would transform our lives. But, as the years went by, our unwavering belief that God would provide at least a modest level of prosperity together with a profound transformation of our sexuality turned out to be lamentably out of touch with reality.

One of the first clear signs that something was seriously awry came in the early years of *Courage* when we were struggling financially. Our astonished accountant challenged me one day. 'Whatever are you doing, giving away all this money?' I explained that we believed we must honour God by giving the first tenth of our income to the church. Tithing was strongly emphasised in those days as a sign of true commitment to God. The corollary of that principle was that God would provide for every need with great generosity. *'Bring the whole tithe into the storehouse, that there may be food in my house. Test me in this,' says the Lord Almighty, 'and see if I will not throw open the floodgates of heaven and pour out so much blessing that you will not have room enough for it.'* (Malachi 3:10) The accountant reacted sharply. 'You are not honouring anyone — you're insolvent.' But I could not countenance such a challenge. The man was not even a believer.

Our duty before God, as we understood it, was to *Wait for the Lord* as the Psalmist urged, and *believe to see the goodness of the Lord in the land of the living* (Psalm 27:13). How could we doubt the leading of the Holy Spirit based on the teaching of the Bible? We were resolved to follow the example of the apostle Peter: when arrested for preaching the gospel and told to stop, he replied, *'We must obey God rather than men'* (Acts 5:29). To do anything less would be to invite God's judgement rather than his blessing.

By the time I realised that the accountant's warning could have been from God, it was much too late to recover financially. From the moment we invested all we had in the ministry, we have struggled on the brink of financial collapse. *The devourer came* anyway. (Malachi 3:11) Of course 'following God's command' could not possibly be wrong. But after many years of relentless financial pressure, and now having lost our home as well, there is no escaping the fact that this personal humiliation has been the result of my own foolish presumption, if not downright stupidity. Commitment to a principle is no excuse for failing to exercise wisdom in financial investment, even when the principle is apparently a biblical one.

But it was intoxicating fantasy to live in a world where, as long as we acted *biblically* and trusted in him, God more or less guaranteed success in everything. Having said that, of course those early years were very exciting. We enjoyed a tremendous sense of community and common purpose. We created a safe place where people could be totally open and honest and bring into the light those shameful aspects of their lives that had been hidden for so long. We believed that our struggles with same-sex attraction were at last going to count for something. We had steadfastly refused to follow the way of the world and felt we could stand with our heads up high, confident that we had a place in God's new kingdom.

In reality, the long-term consequences for many who took part in our discipleship programmes were pretty depressing — near-disastrous for some.

The long-term damage to all of us has been incalculable. A strategy that had largely been inspired by hyped-up charismatic expectations of change proved spiritually catastrophic. Many people gave up their faith altogether. It was financially catastrophic, in that many of us lost practically all we had. It was also mentally and emotionally catastrophic.

The moral consequences have been extremely serious. I can now clearly see that this demand to follow a fundamentalist biblical perspective and refuse to listen to our intuitive sense of what is right, was utterly abusive and morally indefensible. As someone once wittily observed, 'Fundamentalism is not much fun and mainly mental'.

When we celebrated ten years of *Courage* with a special service in London in the summer of 1998, I was privately beginning to experience growing doubts about our direction for the next ten years. The fallout rate of those we had journeyed with was alarming. What had happened to Robert chilled me to the bone as I contemplated the possible consequences of our ministry for the lives of others who I did not know. This turned me back to God in prayer with seriousness and a level of urgency I had never experienced before.

My certainties crumbled as I saw supposedly rock-solid Christian principles bring catastrophe. What I saw challenged my handling of money and my understanding of sexual morality, biblical authority and evangelical Christian teaching. We had been so sure we understood the principles of the Kingdom of God, and sure we knew what the Lord expected of us. As it turned out, we were ignorant of the values of the Kingdom.

Whenever you are dealing with people who know they are right, especially when supported by the word of God, no-one can convince them that they are on the wrong path. Paul's words in 1 Corinthians 6:11 echo in my mind: *Such were some of you.* Hopefully, the tough and humbling lessons of all these years have softened our hearts, teaching us wisdom and understanding of God's ways. Exchanging the actual truth for lies always leads to ruin.

The redemptive aspect of this journey is that I earnestly sought God in a new and deeper way. I discovered more of the human side of Jesus — God incarnate, made man, dwelling amongst us in the flesh — the Jesus who shows to us a new way of living, rather than dictating orders to us from on high. I discovered that Jesus reveals to us the values of the kingdom of God, having made the written code obsolete (Hebrews 6: 8-13). In the kingdom of heaven, compassion feeds the hungry, offers a drink to the thirsty, invites in strangers, clothes the naked and visits people who are sick or in prison (Matt. 25:31-46). Seeking to ascend to the moral high ground and denying what is true for the sake of an abstract ideal — these invite judgement of the severest kind.

James Alison writes,

Ideology is what you have when you don't have faith. When you are *not* aware that there is Another, bigger than us, who is holding all of us in his hand through the upheaval and that ultimately we are safe, there is room, we can be wrong, and we can learn to get it right; when you are *not* aware of that, then you are frightened of disagreement and what you need to do is to produce a unanimity of opinion, of ideology, you need to get everyone to agree, and have those who are in, in, and those who are out, out.

But this is the classic sign of people who have a compulsion for certainty, a compulsion for being right, and a compulsion for being considered to be good, and so who grasp onto a fake certainty, a resolved righteousness, too small a togetherness. If we react like this, then it means that our anchor isn't in the rock beyond the veil. If it were then we would be happy to know that we can all be wrong together, all learn together, and that our squabbling about what is right is a necessary part of the process of all of us learning. In fact, faith in the goodness and trustworthiness of the Creator as revealed by Jesus being prepared to undergo a lynch death and so undo our lynching ways, has as its direct consequence the belief that we can be brought into knowing what is objectively true by the paths of human reason. [4]

From the tough lessons of many years, I too have reached the conclusion that certainty is the very opposite of faith. If you are so absolutely certain of what is right and true, faith becomes obsolete and you cease to see your need for a relationship with God, who is alive. Religious certainty becomes an insidious form of idolatry, the fruit of which is shame and ignominy for its adherents. The only certainty we can rightly hold on to is the assurance of God's grace, his goodness and kindness towards all who turn to him, and his presence amongst us.

4.   Exchanging the truth for a lie

St Paul's words, in the first chapter of his letter to the Romans, describe a people who, in *the sinful desires of their hearts* were given over by God *to sexual impurity for the degrading of their bodies with one another. They exchanged the truth of God for a lie, and worshipped and served created things rather than the Creator.* (Romans 1:25)

For most of my life, along with many evangelical Christian friends whose faith I share, I have believed that this Bible passage gives us God's word about homosexuality and the consequent gay lifestyle. Horrifying statistics have been widely published about promiscuity and disease which, as Christians coming from a conservative viewpoint, we interpreted as plain evidence of the veracity of God's word.

In our ignorance of the real issues, we conveniently overlooked the fact that a persecuted minority is seldom capable of setting and maintaining high moral standards of behaviour. Whatever they do, they are condemned on the basis of who they are. As someone once observed, stories recorded in history are remembered from the viewpoint and interpretation of the victors not the vanquished.

My good friend, Lutheran pastor Māris Sants from Latvia, once left me with a couple of observations that have long stuck in my mind. Having been brought up under a repressive communist government, he realised that when a subject is completely taboo in normal conversation — as Christianity was under the communists, and as life for homosexual people has also been until very recent times — it is impossible to come to any real understanding of the subject. You develop no language among family and friends by which you can come to comprehend it. When someone is considered by society to be an outlaw — because of their faith or their sexual orientation — they are effectively in exile. When an outward testimony of your Christian faith would effectively make you an outlaw and the propagation of the gospel is a criminal offence, how are you to understand your faith?

In the days when homosexuality was a criminal activity, as in the United Kingdom until 1967, there was no way you could openly discuss the subject without fear and come to understand your sexual orientation. So how can you begin to deal with such desires in a healthy way? When under great pressure, you might seek out others of the same orientation in secret, and keep that part of your life hidden from society. But this leads to the destruction of one's self-esteem and any vestige of self-respect as well. Therefore, when an essential self-protective secrecy creates an insuperable stumbling block, how can you even begin to develop an understanding of personal moral responsibility?

In their ignorance of the broader picture, ministries in the United Kingdom such as *Christian Voice* publish statistics claiming to demonstrate the staggering promiscuity of gay men and the high incidence of disease and death in the gay community. They cite such evidence in support of their prophetic message to the nation, warning of the consequences of abandoning the truth, which is that heterosexual marriage or celibacy are the norms for us all.[5] In a similar spirit, the *Christian Institute* publishes the latest trends in government policy, suggesting that the British government is trying to 'force gay rights on churches' and thereby threaten religious liberty.[6] They completely ignore the fact that churches have forced their own agenda on the lives of gay people for centuries, without a thought for the devastation they have caused.

Of course, there are more than a few gay couples around, who have lived for many years in faithful partnerships *(I have listed more than 100 known to me personally at the back of this book, p. 80)*. This includes gay partnerships among professing Christians, including evangelicals, and even among church leaders. These couples are not generally to be found in gay pubs, clubs or saunas. They don't usually have the mental or sexual health problems that would cause their lifestyle to appear in medical records and form the basis of statistical analyses. Because of the extraordinary hostility of society and the church towards gay people, they have learned to live and love discreetly. So it is almost impossible to gather statistics about the kind of gay life that is characterised by love, commitment and faithfulness, because most gay people don't expose the personal details of their partnerships to public scrutiny. They are just ordinary citizens going about their lives like everyone else, tending quite naturally to shun public attention.

5.   We don't wish to know

When I grew up — being a white, English, middle class, educated male — my parents were always very strict about the importance of telling the truth. They would respond with a sharp reprimand if they thought that my sisters or I were telling lies or trying to pull the wool over their eyes.

However, as I grew into my teens, I began to see that not everybody had the same regard for the truth. It shocked me to see that expediency ruled the day among adults I had looked up to and admired. What often began as expressions of tact and human consideration for the feelings of others could soon become complex distortions of the truth. To my dismay, as a teenager, I began to see the truth of Sir Walter Scott's eloquently expressed observation, *Oh what a tangled web we weave, when first we practice to deceive.*

Political and ideological conflicts in everyday life have a way of twisting people's desire to handle the truth with integrity. Similarly, personal agendas and ambitions can so easily cause us to be economical with the truth when it comes to steering our careers in business, Christian ministry and every other area of life. I gradually came to see that inconvenient truths exist, though most people prefer not to speak about them. 'We don't wish to know that', was my father's satirical observation, as he once explained to me the way in which people avoid facing the truth.

Over the years I learned that even evangelical Christians like me, who claim to hold such a high regard for the truth, 'don't wish to know' many things that do not suit their theological viewpoint. They don't wish to know that loving, committed, enduring same-sex partnerships can be rooted in a personal conviction that this also is God's way. This is an inconvenient truth. We preferred to believe the 'horrifying statistics' that 'expose the lie of homosexuality', because they support our biblical contention that homosexuality is wrong and contrary to God's created order. Homosexuals must repent of their 'gay lifestyle' and recognise the truth of God — that we have been created by God as male and female — to be heterosexual, and that 'traditional family values' are the hallmark of the kingdom of God. As a bishop once put it to me, 'If homosexuality is not immoral, then however do you define immorality?' By extension of that logic, homosexual partnerships are a parody of God's creation plan, and all who pursue such relationships are deceived. This was the message of the Bible, as I understood it. I had been taught to read the Bible in this way by the church in which I grew up.

As I went through my teens and started to experience same-sex attractions, I thought there must be something terribly wrong with me. Fearing the possibility that I was deceiving myself, I dared not trust my own judgement or intuition about anything. I lacked confidence and always looked to others, who I perceived as being better than me, to form my ideas and understanding. I became the epitome of a people-pleaser in my desperate attempts to be normal and acceptable to society and the church.

The truth was what better people than me told me it was. The truth was what the Bible taught. And as sinners who can so easily be deceived, when we have a personal interest in seeing things in a way that suits our own agenda, we all surely need to have a high regard for the truth. *Righteousness exalts a nation*, Proverbs 14:34 teaches, *but sin is a disgrace to any people.*

In a fascinating report I recently discovered, from a working party of doctors, nurses and clergy, entitled *Mud and Stars*,[7] it was noted that:

The essence of sin is 'other people telling me who I am and me believing them'. Collusion with inauthentic images of myself can only be a denial of the irreducible originality of the given self, and thus an offence to God. In this sense sin is linked to a great deal of ill-health; for to believe and enact a lie about myself, however unconsciously or for whatever noble motive, can only be conducive to sickness.

So this book is in large part a confession. It is the story of what happens when you doubt yourself so much that you live your life entirely according to the views and rules of others, refusing to recognise or accept the truth about yourself. As I have since discovered, the other way of living — the way of Christ — brings freedom to be all that God intended. But on that journey, along with a great many gay Christians with whom I have travelled, I have had to learn to give up all hope of being able to maintain a good reputation in the eyes of others, and to give up all pretensions of being normal in their sight. I have had to learn to give up all hope of being thought right in my understanding of the truth about God and Christian living as it is taught by the majority of evangelical churches.

The truth, as it is gradually dawning on me now, is infinitely greater than anything I can explain, vastly more complex that anything I can grasp and awesomely more wonderful than my finite mind can ever possibly get hold of. In Christ, God alone is worthy of true worship. I have learned that to live as a man of God and as a follower of Christ means above all to live with personal integrity. I must accept from the outset the truth about myself. And as Christians, discovering that we are gay means facing the truth about ourselves as it is. *This above all: to thine own self be true, and it must follow, as the night the day, thou canst not then be false to any man.*[8] How can we begin to know the truth of God if we deny what intuitively and practically we know to be true of ourselves?

How do we negotiate our way through life when our path is endangered by the minefields of half-truths and explosive lies that can so easily destroy us?

God, as revealed through Jesus Christ, is perhaps best known in popular understanding as the God who is love. But perhaps less well understood, and certainly much less popular, is his humility. As we read in Philippians 2:5-7: *Your attitude should be the same as that of Christ Jesus: who, being in very nature God, did not consider equality with God something to be grasped, but made himself nothing, taking the very nature of a servant, being made in human likeness.*

St Paul tells us that, *since the creation of the world God's invisible qualities – his eternal power and divine nature – have been clearly seen, being understood from what has been made, so that men are without excuse.* (Romans 1:20.) Refusing to recognise what is true about yourself because you fear the opinions of others is a recipe for complete self-deception and takes you on a road to nowhere. Yet when you have no confidence in your own judgement, and when well-meaning people tell you to refuse to believe the lie that you are gay and believe the truth that God made you to be heterosexual, your self-understanding is so profoundly undermined that you begin to feel quite schizophrenic. When you look to others to shape your ideas and under-standing, it becomes ever harder to discern the difference between what is real and what are just received ideas about how things should be. This is how brainwashing operates.

6.   How it might have been

As a young Christian struggling with my sexuality, a close friend who had brought me to Christ introduced me to a local church where I learned a great deal from the pastor's excellent expository Bible teaching. When I first confided in my friend about my struggles, he responded in grave tones, 'Well you know what the Bible says about that.' Some time later, however, he met someone through his work who was a professing gay Christian, living with a male partner. My friend did not know what to make of this, but intuitively he felt that there was something very good about this relationship. He decided to introduce me to them, knowing how greatly I was struggling in myself at the time.

Howard and David were wonderful in their response. They took time to explain to me the struggles they had gone through, and how they had come to realise that God loved them as they were. Moreover, they believed that God had brought them together in response to their prayers. They are still together today over thirty years later. They made no attempt to persuade me of their viewpoint but simply shared their own story in response to my many questions. I was twenty six at that time and would love to have been able to follow in their footsteps. Yet such was my fear of self-deception that I just could not bring myself do so. I feared losing all my friends in church, believing I would probably be excommunicated. I feared losing my career, working as I was for a conservative publishing company. I had no idea how my parents would respond – if they would feel disgusted or ashamed of me. And I had no confidence that I'd ever find a similar relationship. No knight in shining armour was there waiting to ride off with me into the sunset.

Perhaps if there had been just one straight Christian friend who could have said to me, 'I think Howard and David might be right, and I will stand by you if you decide to follow the same path,' I could have done it. But there was nobody. All those who knew me well were clear. This adventure of meeting gay Christians — an oxymoron to them — was a deceptive ploy of Satan and I must shun such a path or face the eternal consequences.

Worshipping regularly at a church that preached a holy God whose wrath against sinful man had been requited by the death of Christ — who loved repentant sinners but warned of the fearful dangers of eternal damnation for those who chose the path of deception — I was constantly reminded of the choices I must make. I believed that the love of God was freely available to all who repented and obeyed. But fearful judgement would be the lot of those who rebelled. The words of the Book of Revelation held me in thrall: *Blessed are those who wash their robes, that they may have the right to the tree of life and may go through the gates into the city. Outside are the dogs, those who practise magic arts, the sexually immoral, the murderers, the idolaters and everyone who loves and practises falsehood.* (Revelation 22:14-15)   Along with my Christian friends, I understood *dogs* to be a euphemism for 'sodomites'.

I dared not risk the possibility of deception. The joy of meeting this gay Christian couple soon faded. The darkness and depression I'd felt for years returned. This was the cross I had to bear — the inevitable price of doing the right thing — or so it seemed. When I wrote and told him of my joyful discovery of 'ex-gay' ministry a few years later, David faithfully wrote back to me and expressed his dismay. It is an extraordinary turn of events that when I needed someone with the time available to edit this book, it has turned out to be David who took on the task, having only just retired from full-time Christian ministry. Clearly God has a great sense of irony.

Frank Sinatra's well-known song *I did it my way* was a great gift to preachers in those days. Many seized the opportunity to declare that this little phrase epitomises man's arrogant and sinful way of living — the refusal to acknowledge any need of God or to accept God's sovereignty over human lives. While the way of the world for people like me was to be gay, the way of the Christian was to live in God's way and struggle against sin.

The point is a perfectly valid one insofar as it presents the challenge of the

Gospel to live a transformed life. But when applied to gay people it has been distorted. In their resolve to seek God's way, preachers have usually failed to recognise the more subtle temptation to pursue a puritanical form of self-aggrandisement that is just another shade of self-deception. No doubt this is why St Paul concluded the argument he started in Romans 1 with the words, *You, therefore, have no excuse, you who pass judgment on someone else, for at whatever point you judge another, you are condemning yourself, because you who pass judgment do the same things.* [9]

7.   Hit and Run Healing Ministry

We had all grown up in a church that believed homosexuality was becoming more widespread and was indicative of the impending collapse of Western civilisation. We did not realise that homosexuality has been around in human society since the earliest times. Its suppression by social stigma did not mean it was not there.   Nor did we realise that homosexuality is widespread in the natural world. [10] We believed it was totally unnatural.

So from our standpoint, it would have been anathema to accept homosexual practice. A few Bible verses strongly reinforced our view — Leviticus 18:20; 20:13; Romans 1:26-27; 1 Corinthians 6:9-11; 1 Timothy 1:9-11. We believed that sexual intimacy was for heterosexual marriage alone. Same-sex partnerships — specifically those that had been consummated sexually — were unthinkable for Christians. We had imbibed the church's teaching that the experience of homosexual desire is a sign of the breakdown of God's creation plan as set out in the book of Genesis. Homosexual practice is indicative of man's rebellion against God. Ignorance of the basic biological facts seriously skewed our perspective right from the start.

Our own experience, however, told us that homosexual people do not voluntarily choose their orientation. On the contrary, if we had been given a choice in the matter, few of us would ever have chosen to be gay. Who relishes the thought of being deemed a sexual pervert by your friends, family and workmates? Knowing for myself how distressing this was, I believe I was called to the pastoral ministry of *Courage* on the understanding that the Gospel offers hope for gay people too, if they earnestly seek to worship God and follow Jesus Christ as Lord.

The way of strict abstinence was not a welcome prospect for most young gay Christian men and women. So some of us sought to become heterosexual, as we believed God intended us to be, in the hope that this would open up the possibility of marriage. At *Courage* we believed this could only happen if it was the heart's desire of the person seeking help. We never sought to help anyone unless they came to us specifically requesting it. They had to come to us with that hope if they wanted to be part of our ministry.

I don't think we really expected to see much in the way of dramatic healing, though we would have loved to see it happen. Perhaps that was indicative of our lack of self-esteem and an underlying fear that God could only bless better people than us. But our sense of hope and expectation was greatly heightened by the claims of healing heard at big conferences and Christian gatherings, such as the popular Bible Weeks held in the UK. Like the woman with the internal haemorrhage (Luke 8:42-48), we hoped to find healing by getting near to Jesus in the crowd, and then slip away before anyone noticed.

Our lack of understanding of homosexuality meant that it was tempting to dismiss sexual orientation as just one of those little problems that a great God can easily deal with. Consequently many of us became conference junkies, attending every Christian conference or Bible Week we could get to. The prospect of encountering a powerful healing ministry from world-class itinerant preachers, healers and bible teachers became addictive. Today's church has the technology and finance to create an amazing atmosphere and sense of theatre, offering a conduit through which the Holy Spirit is invited to come. And if the Holy Spirit does not use the opportunity provided, we can all go home satisfied, having enjoying a tremendous festival of worship.

In the kind of highly charged atmosphere created, the expectations of the faithful are kindled to their peak. The common style of invitation – preached in soothing mellifluous tones by charismatic leaders in moments of such heightened expectation – would go something like this:

> Do you *really desire* ALL that God has for you?
> Do you not know that *God just longs to heal you?*
> Are you sincerely *open to receiving* EVERYTHING that God has for you?
> If so, then just step out in faith . . .come forward to the front . . .
> The ministry team are just waiting in the wings ready to pray for you'.

Time after time we went forward for healing prayer. We longed to be in a position to testify that, 'God has really done something wonderful in my life.' It was such a bore always to be the needy one who never got healed.

Undoubtedly we hungered for the affirmation of our fellow Christians, who would doubtless welcome us as joyfully repentant sinners and who, indeed, genuinely wanted to see an end to our suffering. The peer support was rewarding in itself. When nothing lasting actually happened, we became experts in converting a triumphant sense on *having been healed* to a new spin — that we were *'in the process of being healed'*. This strategy kept us in our traditional theological strait-jacket, so that we never gave up the struggle.

I am quite certain that the preachers were utterly sincere and did not set out to manipulate us. But the striking contrast between accounts of Jesus' healing ministry in the New Testament and what we saw in our charismatic conferences troubled me. Jesus' works of healing were never challenged on the basis that perhaps they had not taken place — on the contrary, the blind *did* see, the lame *did* walk and the dead *were* raised. Not even Jesus' worst enemies suggested anything less; instead, his enemies were riled by the fact that Jesus healing ministry was so obviously effective, because it shamed them, exposed their lack of compassion and undermined their authority.

By contrast, while we enjoyed the eloquent and inspiring words of some very fine preachers, we still had to work hard to persuade ourselves that anything significant had happened at all in terms of actual healing in the long run. With hindsight, clearly it had not. I am not suggesting miracles never happen; I have seen one or two genuine instances myself. But they do not seem to happen to order, and certainly not when we want to make our lives fit a particular social mould, to fit in with the people we look up to.

In the end, it is increasingly hard not to feel that such a preaching style amounts to little more than a confidence trick. Of course it was never intended that way. Travelling preachers seldom have the opportunity to check out the long term results of the promises they are tempted to make so easily, on God's behalf. When a big crowd of hopeful worshippers make on-the-spot claims that God's power has transformed their lives, this is all the evidence of success they needed. But I am left with the feeling that theirs is a hit and run healing ministry, leaving pastors like me to pick up the pieces.

Quite early in my ministry, after a popular speaker from the States who specialises in the 'healing of the homosexual' ran a conference in London, I received a call from a young curate who had given a very bold testimony to having been healed from homosexuality. He had made himself very vulnerable in the process. A few weeks later, he was feeling devastated. 'I got healed at that *(name omitted)* conference', he cried, 'but now I've fallen in love with a guy and I don't know what to do.' I could only listen to him in his distress and pray. I did not possess the charisma of that healer. He lost his faith and left the ministry. I've heard a great many similar stories over the years. It is very hard to cope with such disappointment. And even worse is to hear the hard-liners dismiss such stories with, 'Well of course he cannot *really* have been a Christian can he?' And, 'Young people these days just don't know what it means to have to suffer for Christ's sake'.

8.   Is this the real you?

Much more convincing for me was a testimony I heard at the annual conference of a group in the USA called *Evangelicals Concerned*. There we heard an incredibly moving song called *Is this the real you?* composed by Marsha Stevens of Balm Ministries. [11] The song was inspired by the story of a gifted young man who had given the best years of his life to service in the church, as a youth leader, worship leader and in many other ways.

Because of his unresolved struggle to overcome his homosexuality, there were times when, whilst serving the church, this man had compromised his ministry with some kind of fall into sin. On confessing to his leaders, he was dismissed from his post as youth worker. Time and time again, he had gone forward for healing prayer at Christian conferences in response to the preacher's call, desperately longing to be freed from his homosexual desires and made whole. He was often overwhelmed with depression and a deep sense of failure. He lost all hope for his life as a Christian.

A concerned friend managed to persuade him to go to yet another conference, when a popular visiting preacher with a healing ministry came to town. As the worship began, he felt the old emotions surface, affirming his longing to serve God and his desire not to let the Lord down again. But when the altar call came, he resisted. 'The big question for me Lord is; will I meet with the *real you* this time? I cannot stand another disappointment.' At once, he sensed God speak to him in that still, small voice and with great kindness. 'Son, whenever you have sought me, it has always been the *real me*. The important question is; will it be the *real you* this time?' As he heard God speak to him, he realised that in the past he had always gone for prayer on the basis that he was unacceptable. He had gone forward asking God to make him into someone better. Now it became clear that this was not what God had wanted to do. Previously he had left such meetings disappointed, feeling that God's healing touch had passed him by. Now, for the first time in his life, he realised that God had never wanted him to be any other way – that he was acceptable as he is. Once he realised this truth, he was free to worship and serve God with all his heart – as a gay man.

I found this story, and the song it inspired Marsha Stevens to compose and sing, to be a moment of profound revelation that was very healing. My own hope in God was renewed.

9.　　Problematic Affection

Looking back to the days when we saw the issues in the same way as that young man had done, we whole-heartedly believed that change or healing could be realised through a lifestyle of ongoing repentance, devoted submission to Christ and a willingness to deal with the deeper issues. Our understanding at the time was based to a significant extent on the theories of Cambridge psychologist Dr Elizabeth Moberly[12]. We believed that homosexuality originates from a deficit in normal same-sex bonding, a lack of good role models in childhood and also in a deep need for unconditional love. We therefore believed that non-sexual, therapeutic, same-sex bonding within the Christian community would allow a person to mature into adult heterosexuality and perhaps even go on to marry. The arguments put forward for this approach seemed compelling at the time and many people welcomed our ministry initiative, recognising the pastoral need was great.

However, there weren't many straight men in the church ready to respond with warm-hearted affection to the budding heterosexual masculinity of gay Christian men. Women were generally keener to help. This raised some awkward and unexpected problems at times. The men on the programmes were often well-turned out, sensitive, intelligent and artistic. Single women were naturally cautious. The people with whom the men did bond closely were older married women in the church – surrogate mothers, perhaps. It was easy to see how such relationships fulfilled emotional needs on both sides. The struggling gay man found a sympathetic ear and the woman found warmth and close affection from an attractive younger man. This was disguised as an opportunity for prayer ministry and was apparently all in a good cause. The illusion was that this relationship was safe. After all, the man was gay and the woman was married. In fact, the woman was finding emotional needs met that her straight husband probably knew nothing about and certainly seemed unable to meet. The gay man was finding solace with someone who understood his loneliness and was willing to collude with his homophobic self-hatred. They both agreed that his homosexuality was deviant and needed healing. Some of the pastoral problems that arose were intense and caught us unawares.

There were also some well-meaning heterosexual women in our churches who were surprisingly willing to take their chance with an 'ex-gay' husband. Having fallen in love with 'this lovely man who just had a *little* problem with his sexuality' — nothing too difficult for God to solve of course — they believed that their very genuine and sincere love for their chosen husband could change him and bring the healing God surely wanted to achieve in his life. They were all motivated by the greatest possible concerns for his well-being. In such circumstances, it can be very hard indeed for the gay man who longs to be normal, to be seen as 'healed' and redeemed at last, to resist the temptation to fall in line with the plans other Christians have for him.

For anyone to encourage a gay man to marry a straight woman is at best naive and at worst it causes terrible and long-term suffering to all parties. Too many uninformed Christian pastors and counsellors still seem to believe that all a man needs is a good woman to sort him out. When pastors encourage mixed marriages in this way, they reveal a shameful indifference to the long term outcome for everyone involved. How many pastors would be as happy for their own daughters to marry professing 'ex-gay' men? Would they be so convinced that healing could take place?

Some insights from the creation narrative may be helpful here. In Genesis 3:16 we learn that, from the time of the Fall, a woman would *suffer great pain in childbirth,* yet *she will still have a desire for her husband.* (Presumably the biblical writers thought it superfluous to say that a man will still desire his wife.) Maybe this is why so many pastors assume that any kind of straight sex is good sex, and if it can be contained in heterosexual marriage, so much the better. The astonishing fact is that, after suffering such pain in childbirth a woman does still have a desire for her husband; an amazing sign of the power of love to overcome suffering. But if a woman desires her husband at such cost, the very least she might expect from her husband is that he will reciprocate that desire. It is a very bitter pill indeed to discover that her husband does not desire her much, if at all. And if, later on in marriage, she finds that her husband would rather be with a man, this is about the most devastating message any married woman can receive. But it was at least ten years before we even began to discover this.

10.   Overcoming Addictions

Not all of the men who joined our *Steps Out* programme had been chaste, though many were. Some had lived a double life and become seriously addicted to sexual promiscuity, most often in the form of anonymous one-off sexual encounters. The practice of *cottaging* — meeting other men in public toilets for sex — was not uncommon. Our live-in discipleship houses seemed ideal places for men to come and break that addiction. We provided almost twenty-four-hour accountability. There was openness and honesty and people did not have to hide or live a double life any more. They could admit their sexual contacts and receive understanding, support and prayer for their addictions. Even so, we had no real success in breaking those addictive habit patterns. However much effort we made to hold men accountable for every moment of their day, it made little difference.

One such man was Martin, who had been a highly respected Christian leader in the area he had come from, and who had married — ostensibly very happily. He and his wife really loved each other. Yet his increasingly addictive homosexual behaviour had brought them to a point of crisis. Martin and his wife visited us with a view to his joining our programme. His wife released him for a year to be with us in the hope of restoration for their marriage. Moving to a different area, a long way away from his old familiar haunts, would surely give the opportunity for a fresh start.

Martin was an easy member of our household, very considerate, conscientious and active in applying himself to all we had to offer. Yet after a while his old habit patterns returned. Once he had discovered the local *cottages*, it was not long before he was having frequent sexual encounters again and his addiction reasserted its power. He never failed to confess, but in the end, having applied every strategy known to 'ex-gay' ministry, we were bewildered to know what more we could do to help him.

Not even the experience of a seriously violent assault was a sufficient deterrent. One morning Martin came into my office quite unexpectedly, nursing his bleeding face with his handkerchief and looking badly shaken. I took him to hospital to be checked out and have his wounds properly dressed. It turned out that he had met a man who seemed interested in sex, but on this occasion, Martin had misread the signs. The man led him into local woodland and there proceeded to beat him up. Martin was a tall, solid man — he might have made a good bouncer at a club — but he was a gentle giant who would never have hurt anybody and was certainly not prepared to fight back, even to defend himself. However, even this traumatic experience provided no more than a temporary pause in what had otherwise become a hopeless addiction. When he came to the end of our programme and moved on, we all knew we had completely failed to help him. Unsurprisingly, this brought his marriage to an end.

A year or two later, I learned that Martin had met another gay Christian man and fallen in love. For a while this mild gentle man was uncharacteristically angry and hostile towards us, for continuing what he had come to see as a damaging and abusive ministry. Years later, when we were able to meet and talk about these things, I learned that when Martin had fallen in love, his addiction had been broken overnight. He explained to me that until that point, he had never known what it really meant to be loved, or to be free to express the love he felt for a man who truly cared for him and wanted him. Of course he had experienced Christian love and care from his wife, but we did not accept then that he was actually incapable of a normal heterosexual marriage. He experienced love and care in our community, but the subtle underlying message was that he had always known in Christian circles that love was conditional upon his conforming to what we all believed was right behaviour for a Christian. Once again, experience of *unconditional* love proved that only the real truth has the power to set us free (John 8:31).

Martin's new relationship lasted a little more than a year. His partner was too disturbed by the relentless conflict between his Christian beliefs and his homosexuality to continue in the relationship—a situation we have encountered all too often. Anticipating the flames of hell-fire licking around his ankles just proved too much. Yet this experience of love was sufficient to set Martin free to choose abstinence until he met someone else, with whom he has been in partnership now for many years.

It was to be a long time before I could believe that Martin's experience was acceptable for a true Christian. But the impact was not lost on me. I could see that we were completely unable to deliver on the promise of freedom through belief in the power of Christ alone. The simple love of another man, which was all he had ever really longed for, was easily powerful enough to break the most pernicious of sexual addictions. Eventually, many years later, we were able to agree together that this was truly the work of God in Martin's life. His wife has married again and Martin has recovered his Christian faith, with his partner.

11. Spiritual Castration

In the early 1990s we were unable to see that our best efforts to be a loving Christian community had an abusive edge, because the basis of our thinking was that God's love demands radical obedience. Ten years later, when experience had moved our thinking on considerably, we saw the effects of our former strategy when my wife and I visited some old friends in an 'ex-gay' ministry. The leaders had kindly invited us for dinner with members of their programme. Dinner was followed by an extended worship service. Understandably, telling their programme members about our experience was not on their agenda, but we were deeply touched by their kindness and hospitality. As I sat with this sizeable group of young men, all ardently pursuing the 'ex-gay' programme, a feeling of great sadness came over me. Their worship was so heart-felt and sincere and their commitment to the 'ex-gay' ethos and programme was so dedicated, yet their empty faces revealed a group of men who had been emasculated by the process. They had been taught all their lives that their homosexual desires were deviant and unacceptable to the God who made them. They had devoted all their energy to fighting their sexual desires. They had almost ceased to be recognisably male, such was the devastating effect of this spiritual emasculation.

It is amazing that the barbaric ancient practice of physical castration is today being reproduced so effectively by spiritual and psychological means — and all in the name of Christ. Yet the biblical imperative to be so drastic was deeply embedded in our thinking.

My mind goes to the words of Jesus. *If your hand or your foot causes you to stumble, cut it off and throw it away. It is better for you to enter life maimed or crippled than to have two hands or two feet and be thrown into eternal fire. And if your eye causes you to stumble, gouge it out and throw it away. It is better for you to enter life with one eye than to have two eyes and be thrown into the fire of hell.* (Matthew 18:8-9 TNIV):

Even the most fundamentalist of Bible readers regard these words of Jesus as metaphorical. Clearly we don't see a lot of one-eyed, one-handed, one-footed Christians around, mutilated by their own hand. But undoubtedly Jesus' message is strikingly clear. Allowing any kind of sin — in thought, word or deed — to separate us from God can have devastating eternal consequences and requires decisive action. It was this kind of thinking that drove so many of us to pursue 'ex-gay' ministry.

Jesus did not shrink from presenting some startling metaphors. But the context of Jesus' words should ensure that we are clear about his meaning. Jesus was responding to his disciples' question, *Who is the greatest in the kingdom of heaven?* He called a little child and declared that unless we *take the humble place, like a little child*, we will not enter the kingdom. He goes on to warn against being a stumbling block to faith in Christ. The earlier reference to this metaphor in the Sermon on the Mount, comes in the context of adultery and divorce, revealing how seriously Jesus regarded the tragedy of a broken covenant. (Matthew 5:27-30)

But his words about cutting off limbs or gouging out eyes are surely not terrifying threats to dissuade us from bad behaviour. On the contrary, his words declare a message that a child can easily understand. Children are not generally scared by such shocking imagery, judging by the obvious relish school parties display when taken to visit ghoulish exhibitions like the Chamber of Horrors at Madame Tussaud's waxworks museum in London. Moreover, a child can recognise the comic absurdity of cutting off one hand or gouging out one eye but leaving the other hand or eye to sin with. This would be a futile remedy for sin. Children also understand only too well the tragedy of a broken relationship. Jesus' words point to the tragedy of broken relationship with God, caused by our wilfulness. So unless we understand that our redemption is a loving work of God our Father, simply requiring that we receive his grace with the trusting embrace of a little child, we have understood nothing.

The tragedy of our years in 'ex-gay' ministry is that our pursuit of righteousness with such ardent literalism proved to be a poisoned chalice bringing death not life, and destroying faith rather than nurturing people on their path to life in Christ. Realising our innate mendacity calls for repentance indeed.

12.   Claiming Compassion

In principle, support for ministries trying to heal people from homosexuality showed the compassionate face of the evangelical church at work. The development of ministries in the UK, such as *Courage, Living Waters, True Freedom Trust* and *U-Turn Anglia* (founded by George Harvey, whose son had committed suicide because he was gay and his father had, by his own admission, formerly been homophobic) allowed Christian leaders to refute accusations that they were homophobic. In fact most leaders remained highly dubious about our work and gave us little active or financial support. I suspect they feared the slippery slope — believing that our work was just a covert way of working towards acceptance of homosexuality. So they kept their distance. As it happens, they were right about the long term outcome — but for the wrong reasons.

To many critics, discipleship houses where gay men lived together sounded like a recipe for disaster — conjuring up visions of men facing unnecessary sexual temptation. If they'd ever lived in Christian community, they would have known that, more often than not, people living under the same roof tend to get on one another's nerves. Indeed the great challenge of living in community is to succeed in remaining civil and Christian in one's attitudes.

For most of our church leaders, anything less than a total commitment to change was a soft, self-indulgent option. Perhaps that view has softened, now that more of them realise it is not that simple. But even today, twenty years after the founding of *Courage*, I know of many church leaders who can wax eloquently on the importance of providing acceptance and pastoral care for gay Christians, yet do not lift a finger to help. Every week I meet gay Christians, who have been pushed to the margins of their churches or left out in the cold, disowned by their leaders. This is deeply shocking.

Christ offers us the opportunity to share in his work, commanding us to *love one another as I have loved you. By this shall all men know that you are my disciples, by the love you have for one another.* (John 13:34 -35) Sadly Christ's command receives scant attention when it comes to the pastoral care of gay Christians. The belief that homosexuality is a lifestyle choice, and all that is needed to resolve it is a decision to follow Christ, remains the prevalent view among evangelical leaders today. Gay Christians who come to terms with their sexuality are seen as turning back to a life of sin *as dogs return to their vomit.* (2 Peter 2:22). Our pastoral experience is of no interest whatsoever to evangelicals who think in these terms. They do not realise that they are blind guides (Matthew 23). But for years I was exactly the same. Such people have been my teachers all my life.

13.   Faith in Faith

During the early years of *Courage*, we were very involved in fellowship with other 'ex-gay' groups and with *Exodus International* — a coalition of such ministries. To this day, *Exodus* still preaches a beguilingly simple message:

> "Freedom from homosexuality is to be found
> through the transforming power of Jesus Christ."

There would be no problem with this message if it were true. But as so many 'ex-gay' ministries know perfectly well, this is a very difficult claim to substantiate in the long term. Nevertheless, this was a fresh and popular message at the time of the growing charismatic movement, because it gave hope where there had previously been none.

It felt tremendously exciting to be part of a movement that believed one's life could, in a moment, become a personal demonstration of God's healing power, heralding mighty changes to a tragic, sin-conflicted world. All we needed was faith. I have to say that in those days we all had tremendous faith. With the benefit of hindsight, I realise that what we actually had was faith in faith itself. It was not faith in God, or we would surely have been changed. As with the worship of all idols, biblical or otherwise, we received a miserable dividend. Many could testify to the bitter truth of the Proverb, *Hope deferred makes the heart sick.* (Proverbs 13:12)

Through *Exodus*, I met many 'ex-gay' ministry leaders and their acolytes who, like me, had married. Getting to know many of them quite well personally, and comparing their claimed ministry experience of healing with ours, I realised that the success of all our ministries in the eyes of our churches depended to a very large degree on proving the authenticity of our message by personal example. As married 'ex-gay' ministry leaders, we were the poster boys, and our pay-off was to be lauded as heroes for the cause. It was a very great deal harder for the recipients of our ministry. Most of their marriages have since failed, with the gay spouses subsequently re-identifying with their same-sex orientation.

The most tragic figures in this whole debacle have always been the unfortunate wives of gay men. Though many did not realise it until long afterwards, their needs were totally overlooked. As Carol Grever says in her very helpful book, *My husband Is Gay* [13] :

[After more than thirty years of marriage] the day came when I looked in the mirror and said, 'What's in this for me? What about me!' I finally knew I couldn't spend the rest of my days accommodating someone else's needs at the expense of my own. I had to create a new life for myself. I had to face my fear of loneliness and end our marriage. That moment of insight freed me.

Church leaders haven't the remotest idea how callous it is to encourage gay men to marry with no consideration whatever of the severe trauma this is likely to mean for many wives in the long term. Consideration of the terrible suffering of the wives has been totally neglected.

14.   Laying down the law

A story vividly comes back to mind from the early days of our involvement with *Exodus* which illustrates these dynamics. It encapsulates for me something of the awfulness of what we were doing, though we had no sense or recognition of it at the time.

My wife and I were attending an Exodus conference in the early 1990s. We attended these events as often as we could because they provided the only opportunity we had to find fellowship with others working in the same area of ministry. The encouragement we found there was valuable and empowering for us. Mixing with people who, in being open about their sexuality, were often vulnerable, humble, sensitive and sincere, we shared the difficult journey of striving to do what we believed was right in the sight of God. This kept up our morale. Many of us suffered from very low self-esteem because of the struggle with our sexuality in a hostile society, and we were finding little encouragement for 'ex-gay' ministries in the churches we had come from. Worship at the conferences was always uplifting and the plenary sessions and workshops were inspiring. They provided a great resource for learning as speakers shared their practical experience of ministry. There was really nothing like it to be found anywhere in the world. But, as is so often the case for small groups struggling for their very survival, our capacity for honest and truthful self-criticism was not great.

One morning, we were joined at breakfast by a man who seemed to be in considerable distress—I'll call him Tim. We were joined at once by a psychiatrist committed to developing 'ex-gay' ministry in his part of America. We invited Tim to tell us something of his story and why he had come to the conference. He was clearly desperate to talk. He lived and worked somewhere in the USA, and his work involved a great deal of travelling. He had a wife and son and was a member of an evangelical church. What none of them knew was that he had a male lover in Mexico and stayed with him when business trips allowed. Tim was feeling very unhappy and frightened. 'I have come here to get my life sorted out', he blurted out, sounding desperate. Some time back, he had confessed his homosexuality to his wife and to his local church leaders. His wife had threatened that if he fell again she would divorce him. His church threatened excommunication. His son somehow knew, and despised him. So for Tim to admit to them that a covert relationship had begun did not augur well for the prospect of reconciliation with his family or church.

The psychiatrist, who can only have been half listening, did not waste a moment in telling Tim, in forthright terms, that he must give up the affair with the Mexican at once. 'You must write and tell him you will never see him again', he insisted. Tim seemed very distressed by this advice, protesting that he could not simply write a letter to end it. He felt that he must face the man and explain why he was breaking up their relationship. 'No! No!' the psychiatrist protested, 'You are not strong enough to maintain your resolve to give up this sinful relationship. You will only be drawn back in. You must write without further delay and bring an end to it once and for all.' Tim's prevarication prompted further instructions, including the insistence that he must confess everything to his wife and church leaders. This would demonstrate that he was fully repentant and genuinely prepared to get his life in order. He must make himself accountable to people who could help to keep him from falling again. He must also give up the career that provided such opportunities for sin.

My wife and I were frankly embarrassed at this strident and bullying tone of counsel. Such a controlling style was not in itself new to us. Perhaps it is just that, in the UK at least, people are usually more covert in using it and are less obviously offensive. Tim looked ready to choke before he'd even taken a mouthful of breakfast.

There was a brief pause in the tirade of advice, and I ventured to ask Tim gently, 'Is it possible that the reason for your reluctance to give up your affair with the Mexican guy is that you are in love with him?' The dam burst. The poor man broke down in floods of tears and was inconsolable for the next twenty minutes. Fortunately, the psychiatrist had other things to do and left us — to our mutual relief. No doubt he wanted to make himself available to advise someone more receptive.

When Tim had calmed down sufficiently, I said slowly and gently, 'It looks as though you are facing a no-win situation. If you confess to your church, they've already threatened to excommunicate you. If you confess to your wife, she has promised to divorce you, and your son will just despise you all the more. If you give up your job without having found a new career, you will lose your source of income. And if you give up your lover in Mexico, you will lose the love of the man you clearly find so precious. There is only one person I know who can help you in this situation. He shares your concern for your wife and family — in fact he loves them more than you do. He knows how important it is for a wife to have a husband who is faithful, whom she can trust in and rely on. He knows how important it is for a son to have a Dad he can look up to and admire. He knows what it means to have to face real temptation and to struggle with it desperately. He loves you and he understands your weaknesses and all your sorrows right now. I am sure you already know the one of whom I speak — his name is Jesus. Right now there is only one thing I believe Jesus would ask of you — that you turn to him, relax and begin to enter into his peace. There you can begin to discover his unconditional love for you. Because until you come to that place of peace in your own heart, you cannot begin to make important decisions that are bound to have major life-changing consequences. When you find that place of peace with Christ, you can begin to work out together what you must do next.' Tim calmed a little in hearing my words.

I saw him later at the conference, again looking wild-eyed and fearful. That kind of environment only reinforced the psychiatrist's advice. I suggested, 'Don't be too hasty to ask advice of just anyone willing to offer it. Only the peace of Christ will enable and empower you to find the way forward.' But he looked to me like a man who did not believe he could make any decisions for himself. He was desperate to find someone who would be strong enough to make decisions for him. Like most of us, he wanted someone with skin on to tell him what to do and to walk with him, not someone whose love and discipline he had to accept by faith. I never saw him after that.

The importance of learning to just listen and walk alongside our brothers and sisters in the journey of faith without feeling we must always offer advice is incalculable. Jesus surely gave us this example in his ministry again and again, but at no time more memorably than when, after his resurrection, he walked unrecognised with two disciples along the road to Emmaus (Luke 24). The importance of this is powerfully portrayed in the words of Dietrich Bonhoeffer, in his book, Life Together[14], published just before the outbreak of the Second World War. These words are amazingly pertinent for our present time:

The first service that one owes to others in the fellowship consists in listening to them. Just as love to God begins with listening to his Word, so the beginning of love for the brethren is learning to listen to them. It is God's love for us that he not only gives us his Word, but also lends us his ear. So it is his work that we do for our brother when we learn to listen to him. Christians, especially ministers, so often think that they must always contribute something, when they are in the company of others, that this is the one service that they have to render. They forget that listening can be a greater service than speaking.

Many people are looking for an ear that will listen. They will not find it among Christians because these Christians are talking when they should be listening. But he who can no longer listen to his brother will soon be listening no longer to God either; he will be doing nothing but prattle in the presence of God too. This is the beginning of the death of the spiritual life, and in the end there is nothing left but spiritual chatter and clerical condescension arrayed in pious words. One who cannot listen long and patiently will presently be talking beside the point and be never really speaking to others, albeit he be not conscious of it. Anyone who thinks that his time is too valuable to be spent keeping quiet will eventually have no time for God and his brother, but only for himself and his own follies.

Brotherly pastoral care is essentially distinguished from preaching by the fact that, added to the task of speaking the Word, there is the obligation of listening. There is a kind of listening with half an ear that presumes already to know what the other person has to say. It is an impatient, inattentive listening, that despises the brother and is only waiting for a chance to speak and so get rid of the other person. This is no fulfilment of our obligation, and it is certain too that here our attitude towards our brother only reflects our relationship to God. It is little wonder that we are no longer capable of the greatest service of listening that God has committed to us, that of hearing our brother's confession, if we refuse to give ear to our brother on lesser subjects. Secular education today is aware that often a person can be helped merely by having someone who will listen to him seriously, and upon this insight it has constructed its own soul therapy, which has attracted great numbers of people, including Christians. But Christians have forgotten that the ministry of listening has been committed to them by him who is himself the great listener and whose work they should share. We should listen with the ears of God that we may speak the Word of God. [14]

Thinking back over Tim's story again, I am reminded of the crucial importance of the incarnation. In Jesus Christ, God came to dwell among us as a man—with skin on—and revealed what it means for us to love one another. No wonder it was so hard for Tim to renounce his Mexican lover. All he got from well-meaning 'ex-gay' Christians was the assurance of remaining an outcast if he failed to comply with the rules. The fact that Tim was so unhappy about writing to terminate the relationship suggests that he really loved the man. They were not merely partners in lust. I would like to think that he did not renounce the man he loved, but that he went back and that they are now living happily ever after. But this is an unlikely scenario, if only because Tim would have been too full of inner conflict to accept such a relationship, even if their love was mutual. At the very least he would have had to reject his understanding of the Christian faith, otherwise he would have remained bound up in condemnation. Very few relationships are able to withstand for long the relentless hostility meted out by the church. Who can cope with the unending condemnation that churns up our consciences, denying us all human dignity, self worth and self-respect because of the wretchedness we are made to feel about being gay.

Tim's story encapsulates many pastoral situations we have faced over the years. Laying down the law is the easiest way out for pastors who feel out of their depth. After telling people the right thing to do with their lives, pastors can just walk away and leave them to get on with it. If they succeed, then the pastor's ministry is vindicated; if they fail, then they are deemed to be backsliders who have no hope unless they repent. From the church's point of view, it can become a smug case of 'we win, you lose'. That sounds very like the ministry style of the Pharisees and teachers of the Law.

15.   Holy betrayal

In the early years of the *Courage* ministry, a mature woman came to see me who had totally lost confidence in her church leader. She had been a highly respected member of the ministry team in a large charismatic church. What none of them knew was that she was experiencing struggles over her sexuality. Eventually she plucked up the courage to confide in her vicar. To her horror, it soon became obvious that he had discussed their conversation with the rest of the ministry team without consulting her. She confronted him saying, 'But I spoke to you in confidence', to which he lamely replied, 'Confidentiality isn't a New Testament principle'. I was shocked to hear this. The word *confidentiality* may not be found in the text of the New Testament, but surely Jesus' words *Do to others what you would have them do to you* (Matthew 7:12) include the principle of confidentiality out of respect for the person who makes themselves vulnerable. I wonder how trustworthy the minister would have been in hearing people's confessions where absolute confidentiality must always be assured.

The scale of betrayal and the breaches of confidentiality I have witnessed are so horrendous that at times it makes me ashamed to call myself a Christian.

Because of the damage done, I believe I must draw attention to a practice that is so often sanitised with a claim to be upholding principles of holiness.

I have listened to plenty of true stories like the one that follows. A mature married man — the greatly loved leader of a large and thriving fellowship that he has devoted his life to building up — was struggling increasingly with feelings of same-sex attraction, that he had never acted upon. Not knowing where to go for help, and realising that he would be putting other leaders in the church in a difficult position if he were to tell them, he spoke to a close friend he felt sure he could trust. His friend seemed unperturbed and was reassuring. He prayed for him. The minster felt that a huge burden had been lifted from his shoulders. But clearly the burden had been too great for his friend. Twenty-four hours later, the minister was summoned to a special meeting of the church elders. He was given a choice. He must accept three months salary and leave the district with his family at once. He must attend no further church meetings and he must not speak to anybody from the church. The alternative — not expressed in these terms of course — was that he would be publicly outed and summarily sacked for moral failure without another day's pay. He was told he must decide there and then; no time was allowed for him to think about it. With a wife and family to provide for, the choice is simple — you take the salary and leave. Some stay on to protest. Either way, the long term consequences are devastating for everybody. Long ago, I lost count of the number of ministers who have come to me with stories that go something like that one.

Another less fortunate minister — the pastor of a church from a somewhat stricter evangelical tradition — was much loved by his congregation. He, too, had built up a thriving fellowship of new converts in only a few years, having started with just a handful of elderly folk. When he found he could no longer cope with his unspoken feelings of same-sex attraction, he told his wife. Naturally she felt alone, frightened and upset. Nevertheless she loved her husband and wanted to work out what was the best course for them both. After praying and talking things through over several weeks, they agreed that it would be best to separate and, in due time, to divorce. They were duty bound to tell the church leadership about their plans. He had never acted on his feelings of same-sex attraction; he just did not know what to do with his struggles. Fortunately he had contacted me first and he had our prayer support. He shared his situation privately with the leading elder. Within hours, he was summoned to a specially convened emergency leadership meeting, where he was summarily excommunicated. The church quibbled over his final salary payment and he was not even allowed to return to the manse to collect his clothes or personal belongings. At this extraordinary meeting, as he turned to leave, he was overwhelmed by the Holy Spirit and walked out—with nothing left but the clothes he stood up in—singing Psalm 23 *The Lord is my shepherd*, to the astonishment of all present. His wife was immediately approached by the leadership and told to have nothing further to do with her husband, as he was deemed to be a tool of Satan. She would be better to distance herself from him totally. She was in a frightening position.

This took place in very recent years. The pastor would have been fully protected by employment legislation. But because he had a deep pastoral concern for his congregation, he did not want to drag the church through the courts. As a Bible-based Christian leader, he knew St Paul's admonition that Christians should not take one another to court, so he never defended himself. (1 Corinthians 6)

He was left homeless and without a penny, with no training for any career outside the ministry. He found a job filling shelves at a local supermarket where he earned a pittance, yet he did his utmost to continue to support his wife financially, though he was able to have minimal contact with her. As an educated man who had devoted his life to the pastoral care of others, I greatly admired his willingness to get on and do any job available. With nowhere to live, cut off from his friends and family, he visited a gay pub for the first time in his life. There he met a man who had a spare room to offer. Within a short time, they fell in love and have subsequently become committed partners. He has never lost his hope in Christ and continues to share his faith whenever he finds the opportunity. The big problem comes when he has to recommend a church to which new believers can safely go.

Another man who stayed with *Courage* for a while, came from Northern Ireland. He had been a wealthy businessman and by far the biggest contributor to his church through his tithes and offerings. When he confessed to the leadership that he had fallen in love with another man at work and been unfaithful to his wife, he was excommunicated at once. This must have cost the church dearly in lost money. However they soon made sure that the whole community knew. His entire business collapsed for lack of trade and he went bankrupt. He told me that in Northern Ireland it was more acceptable to be a murderer than a homosexual. One of the church elders involved in the case told him, 'I committed adultery once', — he spoke with a shudder — 'but at least it was with a woman'.

If the situation is bad for Christian leaders working in the UK, it can be even worse for missionaries. Another man we know, who had worked for twenty years in the Middle East for a missionary organisation, had married and raised a family, but suppressed his feelings of same-sex attraction because he believed they were wrong. But the tough and lonely struggles of working on the mission field in a very hostile environment eventually became too much for him. When he confessed to being in a compromising position with another man, he and his family were sent back to the UK on the next flight. He was summarily dismissed by the missionary organisation, without a day's further pay. His bewildered wife, dealing with her own feelings of shock and betrayal, was left to fend for herself and the children. As usual, *their* needs were not given a moment's consideration. He had then passed forty and had training for nothing else so he had no means of providing for his family. He subsequently trained for a new career, which he began a couple of years later inevitably on a minimal salary. I asked if he had any regrets after the traumas he had been through. His wife had married again, and he simply replied that at last he felt he could be truly himself.

What is it that makes churches feel able to act without the least concern for employment law or even show the rudiments of common decency to those who have served them well for many years? The subject of homosexuality evidently creates such shock waves in their lives that it gives them *carte blanche* to terminate all contact. It seems that they have to do this to protect themselves, their reputations and apparently their congregations from becoming spiritually infected. The fear that the devil has come into their midst and made the whole church vulnerable to God's judgement runs very deep. Of course, the biblical call to holiness is usually cited as the reason. No matter that Jesus spent his time with tax collectors, prostitutes and sinners. Jesus was only doing that, apparently, to give them an opportunity to be converted and live a redeemed life. Is it that Christian leaders who fall should know better and must expect to be dealt with more harshly? After all, the Bible does say that leaders will be judged more severely.

Nevertheless, the church in the West can appear to be the epitome of mercy compared to other parts of the world. In some African countries, the persecution of gay people by Christians has reached the most horrifying proportions. I have pictures in my office of an African lesbian Christian who suffered an acid attack at the hands of her accusers. It is not that she was openly gay, but simply that she lived with another woman, and when two people love one another very deeply, it can be hard to conceal. When they were attacked by a group of do-gooders seeking to expunge this evil in their midst, her partner was killed. Although she herself survived, she was horribly disfigured. The leader of the small gay Christian group of which she was a member sent us the pictures, asking us to remember them in our prayers.

It seems extraordinary that hard-line preachers should spend so much time denouncing Western governments who give legal recognition to loving same-sex partnerships, declaring that this will bring God's judgement on our nations. At the same time, just out of sight and clearly out of mind, male rape is a regular occurrence among our prison populations, perpetrated by frustrated heterosexual men, many of whom will go back to their wives on release from prison[15]. It never seems to occur to those preachers that their energies might more fruitfully be used in the name of Christ to campaign for prison reform, instead of attacking gay men and lesbian women who want to make a commitment to one another out of mutual love. Homophobic fear based on ignorance clearly runs very deep in all cultures to this day. The church should take seriously the fact that its anti-gay rhetoric contributes to the level of homophobic violence in our society.

16.   The pursuit of holiness

Towards the end of the 1990s, I had become increasingly aware that 'ex-gay' ministries, especially in the USA, were too afraid to assess honestly the fruit of their work and admit their staggering level of failure.   European ministries were a little more open.   I remember being strongly criticised by one 'ex-gay' ministry leader in the USA for our lack of faith, and being told how much we dishonour God as a result. In reality, if these people had been running a business that depended for its survival on the quality and reliability of their product, they would have become bankrupt years ago. If they had been offering a medical solution for some sickness or disease and had produced as disastrous a long term effect on their patients as we had, they would have been sued out of existence. Yet none dared risk expressing their own disappointment for fear of losing the meagre financial support that came from their evangelical churches.

Over the years of my involvement, the semantics of the *Exodus* message have been regularly massaged to respond to each new wave of criticism. Looking at an *Exodus* website today as I write, I notice that the message has been subtly tweaked to say, 'We are not proclaiming that heterosexuality is the answer to homosexuality, but rather that holiness is the answer'. Does this mean that the pursuit of holiness makes human relationships redundant? Should heterosexuals renounce marriage from now on to pursue holiness? Is a relationship with God alone sufficient? Well, it wasn't considered sufficient in the perfect world of the Garden of Eden. As far as I am aware, nothing has happened since to change that conclusion.

At *Courage*, we believe in the pursuit of holiness too, but our understanding of holiness is that it means that Christians seek God and live lives set apart for the service of God in their communities. But holiness is never defined by whether or not we have sex with the person we love — a person to whom we are faithful and committed in relationship before God.

The trouble is that we all felt caught between the devil and the deep blue sea. The devil offered incentives to pursue a lifestyle of all-consuming lust and addiction leading to devastation and ruin — especially when you were young and gorgeous-looking. The church offered us love, on condition we remained celibate or, even better, if we played the marriage card and jumped for joy about it on their public relations bandwagon. For most of us, this was the deep blue sea. This can be a very lonely place in which to live.

I came to the point where I could no longer collude with what I felt was the dishonesty of my fellow 'ex-gay' ministry leaders. Well-meaning though I knew them all to be, their message was plainly false. The *Exodus* board saved me the trouble of resigning when they terminated *Courage's* membership at their conference in the summer of 2000. I had no regrets about leaving. Expulsion did me a favour. My greatest regret was my own mendacity in cooperating with it all for so long, and the fact that I had not acted to distance myself much sooner.

I have been told often enough that my 'commendable pastoral heart of compassion' has blinded me to the biblical call to holiness. If this is so, I prefer the kind of blindness I suffer from to the myopic vision so evident among those who pursue holiness on own their terms. On the day of judgement, I would much prefer to be called to account for erring on the side of compassion. The kind of holiness these preachers talk about sounds terrifying and, to my mind, is entirely inconsistent with the ministry of Jesus as described in the Gospels. Pursuing holiness through indifference or betrayal is an oxymoron if ever there was one.

17.   Treasures old and new

We can all applaud the courage of people who have come to terms with a handicap of one sort or another. Vividly imprinted in my mind is the amazing story of thalidomide survivors told on television in a documentary directed by Benetta Adamson some years ago [16]. They demonstrated astonishing courage in coming to terms with their handicap and finding ways to make their lives work well. I remember the interviewer talking to a middle-aged lady in a motorised wheelchair, who had stumps for arms and legs yet steered her vehicle using her chin with great expertise down the supermarket shopping aisles. Having married and raised a family, she was shopping to celebrate her daughter's birthday. The interviewer asked if she resented having been crippled by the effects of the thalidomide drug, and the disfigurement that made her look gauche compared with her rather attractive daughter. 'Oh no,' she declared with a robust laugh, 'this is the real me. If anyone has difficulty with me or my appearance, then that's their problem not mine.' It is interesting to recall some of the other observations made by thalidomide survivors on that programme:

> "It's not me that is the problem, it's the way that society defines me."
> or "We *are* normal—just different."

When anyone learns to see their handicap as an opportunity to rise up, overcome challenges and learn to live well, we marvel at their courage. Yet when gay people have the courage to embrace their sexuality as a gift from God and learn to live and love well as gay Christians, they are seen as taking the easy option, and settling for the broad road to destruction (Matthew 7:13). What is recognised as a virtue in one set of circumstances is judged a vice in another. And what is indisputably courageous in one context is treated as a satanically- inspired conspiracy by our churches.

Sometimes the simplest answers in life are the least obvious to us. Our lives so easily become complicated with hidden agendas—hence the need to become like little children. I have seen the truth of this over and over again during my lifetime, yet I still find it difficult to put into practice myself. Why are we all so slow to learn? Undoubtedly our innate sinfulness blinds us to the obvious. As Isaiah and Jesus pointed out: *You will be ever hearing but never understanding; you will be ever seeing but never perceiving. For this people's heart has become calloused; they hardly hear with their ears, and they have closed their eyes. Otherwise they might see with their eyes, hear with their ears, understand with their hearts and turn, and I would heal them.'* (Matt. 13:10-15)

Jesus' disciples had left their jobs and their synagogues — all their comfort zones — to follow him. Those who stayed with Jesus, when all the rest had gone home, had the meaning of the parables explained to them. It follows that, when we place our hope in anything other than the God who, through Christ, works to be reconciled with us, we end up expending all our energies following blind guides. Unsurprisingly we find ourselves led up blind alleys and facing brick walls. However sincere or well-meaning we are, we have altogether missed the point. None of us seems to be immune.

Perhaps this is just the difficult road to Christian maturity, but there must be an easier way. At a conference I attended last year, the Franciscan writer, Fr Richard Rohr, commented that *if God cannot get our attention through the message of his love, then he gets our attention through suffering.* And the fact has to be faced that much of our suffering has been of our own making.

Over the past twenty years, it has been a tremendous privilege to work with some of the most dedicated Christians I have ever met. We worked with many sincere, God-fearing folk, especially during the toughest first ten years of our ministry. I often thought in those days that if the average church member showed the kind of commitment to Christ that I saw amongst Christians struggling with their sexuality, we would transform the world. Yet now I wonder. If we had succeeded in our objectives we would more likely have been paving the road of a hell of our own design — a kingdom ruled by a totalitarian government of Christian thought police who set out to monitor and guide every thought and action. Only those rebels who were prepared to sacrifice their reputation and even die would escape and go to heaven. Mercifully, Jesus Christ works among us to subvert our sinful ways.

As gay Christians, we believe in the Bible as God's Word, and accept Paul's words to Timothy that *all Scripture is God-breathed and is useful for teaching, rebuking, correcting and training in righteousness, so that the man of God may be thoroughly equipped for every good work.* (2 Timothy 3:16-17) To me, *God-breathed* and *useful* suggest a living word, confirming the new covenant in which God promises to speak personally to our hearts and minds by his

Spirit, just as he spoke to Moses, Paul and all the biblical writers. 'Useful' is not a word that implies 'mandatory'.[17] The challenge for us all is to believe what God says to us, even when that creates conflict with those who don't see things in the same way. Christian discipleship requires us to get over the hurt when we lose our credibility in the eyes of others, and to go on trusting in God anyway.

When we face great pressure, we can be tempted to give up the struggle or we are driven to seek God in the midst of that pressure. It is amazing how in seeking God we discover *treasures old and new* — as similarly dedicated straight brothers and sisters will know (Matthew 13:52). Again and again, in our great need, we turn to the Bible to see what hope we can glean.

Among those treasures, the gay person discovers the tender compassion of God towards all who seek him; the affirmation of eunuchs (Isaiah 56 and Matthew 19); the celebration of a same-sex covenant between Jonathan and David — the man after God's own heart (1 Samuel 18 & 20); the evident freedom they had to lavish affection upon one another without inhibition (1 Samuel 20); David's subsequent grief at the death of Jonathan in battle, prompting words of unashamed love and tenderness (2 Samuel 1); the fact that Jesus could openly love another man without courting reproach even from enemies who earnestly sought reason to destroy him (John 13; 20-21). The offence taken by some Christians because we might be implying a gay element to such relationships is a red-herring. The simplicity and beauty of their love for one another speaks to all who are open to understand.

There are many passages calling us to shun sexual immorality but one has to ask the question, 'What could the term immorality have meant to the writers of the Bible?' They must have had a very different perspective from ours, because the practice of polygamy and concubinage was widespread in those days, without condemnation. We see the concession to divorce, and an extraordinary lack of clarity as to what actually constitutes a legal marriage. Even Solomon was not criticised for having seven hundred wives and three hundred concubines (1 Kings 11:3), though he was judged for allowing some of them to lead him into idolatry.

A strong sense of moral responsibility towards our neighbour remains at the core of our values. But since we could not find a mention of celibacy anywhere in the Bible, inevitably we began to question whether this was God's demand or a doctrine of man.

18.   Demanding Celibacy

I was always taught, unequivocally, that *God's standards are absolute chastity before marriage and absolute fidelity after marriage.* These impassioned words from my pastor are still ringing in my ears thirty five years later. So celibacy is demanded of all single people in the Church – whether they have never married or are widowed or divorced. To suggest that gay Christians should be treated any differently sounds like special pleading[18], an accusation that I believe is unjustified, but when proffered tends to oppose any discussion.

Loneliness is never easy to cope with. But evangelical gay Christians have been left with no option other than to be single. I know a number of older women who have been able to marry later in life, after a long period of singleness. They may have married too late to have children, but they are still able to enjoy many years of happiness with their husbands, and everyone rejoices for them. But who among our conservative Christian leaders rejoices when a gay man or woman finds a same-sex partner they love? Usually they are given an ultimatum; give up this relationship or give up fellowship with this church.

The tempting serpent in the Garden of Eden is famous for having deceived with words, *Did God really say . . .?* And we all know that God did indeed forbid eating the fruit of the tree of knowledge of good and evil. The serpent was challenging the integrity of God's word. When we ask, *did God really say no to same-sex partnerships,* the straight world imposes a number of texts upon us which clearly have to be twisted to make them into a prohibition against committed partnerships. We are also told that not only must we not have same-sex partnerships, we must be totally celibate, because sex is for straight people who are married. And of course, in polite Christian parlance, straight married people don't actually have sex – they make love. Only unmarried people have sex – a clever use of words that betrays the mixed metaphors we use to rubbish relationships that we believe do not fit the accepted norm. Our choice of words associates one group with lust, whilst exalting those relationships that fit the traditional model. Any of us can slip into using loaded language, yet we also know that heterosexual marriages are sometimes unloving, abusive and doomed to failure.

When we search the scriptures for ourselves, we find that the picture is not so clear cut. What we do see is that the choice to *renounce marriage for the sake of the Kingdom of Heaven* was recognised by Jesus (Matthew 19:12) and supported by Paul (1 Corinthians 7:7). But both are quite clear. Singleness is a gift and the decision to renounce marriage stems from a call to set aside the heavy responsibilities of raising a family and to devote oneself to the kingdom of God. This was a very radical idea in Jesus' day when raising children was of immense social importance.

Jesus' use of the word *eunuch* [19] in Matthew 19 simply describes a person unable to marry for some reason. Unable to marry usually meant being infertile, hence qualifying a castrated eunuch to serve in the harem of a king. But it certainly does not mean, or even imply, being incapable of having any kind of sexual relationship. Nor is the word *eunuch* a synonym for celibacy. In fact, no prohibition against sexual intimacy is implied at all in Jesus' words. The notion that celibacy is a requirement has been quite falsely read into the passage; it is simply not there.

In the days when the infant mortality rate was high and life expectancy was short, raising children was a great social necessity. That is not the case today. The essential foundation for heterosexual marriage in society has radically changed. Today, mutual love and desire to be with the spouse of your choice is the basis of marriage, and these reasons have superseded the social imperative to raise children.

Moreover, the practice of birth control has gained widespread acceptance, in spite of vigorous protests in the church just seventy years ago about it being unnatural. There is no biblical authorisation for the acceptance of birth control. The justification, as it has been explained to me, is that birth control is permissible because God first created marriage for companionship and secondly for procreation. (Amazing how heterosexual bible teachers can find ways around the scriptures.) In such circumstances, honouring God in glorious heterosexual companionship, birth control allows for responsible family planning in a world where it has become very expensive to provide for a rapidly growing family. This never seems to have been a worry for people in Bible times however poor they were. On the contrary, the more children a couple had, the more support they were likely to have in a world without pension schemes. Those who were childless had good reason to be worried about their old age, unless they were wealthy.

If it is true that birth control has become acceptable for Protestant Christians over the last seventy years — contrary to nature though this clearly is — and if marriage was given by God for companionship first and secondly for children, where is the argument against gay people enjoying the same commitment and intimacy?

The jury is still out as to the underlying causes of homosexuality, but while there's very little evidence of a psycho-dynamic explanation, there is increasing evidence that homosexuality is congenital and fixed very early, probably in the womb. All the scientific evidence that has come to light in the past ten years strongly suggests that sexual orientation is real, innate and not man-made.[20]

Perhaps Jesus' words about eunuchs have actually rendered the debate irrelevant. There is a place in the kingdom of God for eunuchs who serve God, for whatever reason they do not marry. Indeed, Jesus' words indicate that *seeking first the kingdom of God* is the most important goal. The message is reinforced by his very next words; *Let the little children come to me, and do not hinder them, for the kingdom of heaven belongs to such as these.* (Matt 19:14)

19.   Reasons to Hope

Ten years ago, we began to ask ourselves what basis we had for continuing to insist that those coming to *Courage* comply with their churches' demands for all unmarried people to remain celibate. Under continual pressure to renounce same-sex relationships based on mutual love and commitment, and with no viable alternative on offer, we ceased to have confidence in the authority of the church's teaching about this. We found no instruction from the Bible to substantiate the command.

Yet the burden of guilt for desiring a companion of the same-sex has remained for many because we are surrounded by voices that tell us it is sin. For this reason I have seen a great many folk become profoundly disillusioned. So many have become seriously depressed and hopeless, and some are unable to work or function normally. This should be evidence enough that something is seriously wrong. Secular counsellors have no difficulty at all in recognising this, but too many Christian leaders dismiss their views because they are not Christian. As a pastor committed to helping people find their hope in Christ, I find this situation heart-breaking, as I have seen some folk become suicidal and others lose their faith.

In striking contrast, I see that those gay Christians who have embraced the possibility of a same-sex relationship have greatly benefited. It is malicious and defamatory to interpret their desire merely as a lascivious craving for sex. To represent erotic intimacy between gay people in this way gravely misjudges the situation. The truth is that when gay people really love one another, sex is only the icing on the cake. It is not the substance of the relationship. This is true for straight people too. Gay partnerships, entered into sincerely with mutual commitment, provide the same value and sense of belonging as marriages. And when Christ has central place, people's morale — above all their hope in God — recovers.

Scripture teaches that *the joy of the Lord is our strength* (Nehemiah 8:10). Why believe church leaders who teach us that we are pariahs unfit for the kingdom of God, who rob us of the joy they find in Christ, and in marriage?

Courage has always been a pioneering ministry and not a militant group fighting for gay rights, so it was a daunting prospect to consider embracing a gay affirming outlook. Working out a new mandate for our ministry was fraught with problems. I worried greatly that we might find ourselves inadvertently licensing an 'anything goes' approach. But we had learned a number of very important lessons over the years and found reasons to be confident in our new direction.

Firstly, we knew that we are all called to a personal relationship with God in Christ and we may reasonably anticipate that God will reward our seeking of him. We can go to God directly in our own right and God draws us to seek him. (John 6:44)

Also, in our charismatic churches, we were taught to expect the Holy Spirit to come, not only to change our hearts but also *to guide us into all truth* (John 16:13). This belief had been important for many early leaders in the charismatic movement who had known what it was like to be shunned by traditional churches. Once pushed out on their own, charismatic leaders had to have confidence in the leading of the Holy Spirit, and theirs was the example we had learned to follow.

This in turn gave us increased confidence in our prayer life. Why should we doubt we were hearing the voice of God when we earnestly sought him? And when deep down in our hearts we sensed God's acceptance and approval of our same-sex desires, more and more of us became confident in accepting we are gay. We became reassured that our desire for committed relationship is as legitimate as for our heterosexual brothers and sisters.

As we began to find the courage to speak out about our convictions, we received affirmation from some surprising quarters of the church. Privately, an increasing number of evangelical leaders expressed their support for our new approach. By no means did we lose the support of our evangelical brethren entirely. Contrary to some expectations, however, we did not find support for our change of view from the secular gay community. Many gay people simply dismissed us as insane for our continuing association with homophobic religion.

As we studied the Bible for ourselves, not only did the traditional 'clobber texts' lose credibility because they clearly did not apply directly to those of us who'd spent our lives seeking God, but we also found many other passages that affirmed and supported us as people for whom heterosexual marriage is not appropriate as same-sex commitment is.

For those of us who had come from strictly evangelical backgrounds where we had learned from brilliant authoritative Bible teachers in the past, God provided succour from Dr Roy Clements — a Bible expositor *par excellence* — who, with his renowned teaching skills and authority as a world class Bible teacher, has supported our change of approach.

We also learned of the ministry of *Evangelicals Concerned* [21], founded in the USA by Dr Ralph Blair in 1975, at around the same time as the 'ex-gay' movement began. He once explained to me that when he first became a Christian, he realised that — if it is true that we are saved by faith in what Christ has done, then the anti-gay message *cannot* be true. Whether we are straight or gay is irrelevant to God's redemptive work in our lives. It is the fact of our responding to Christ that is the all-important thing.

This theologically conservative group of evangelical gay Christians had much to share with us out of their long experience. At their conferences we have met many people who are in long-term partnerships, giving the lie to the notion that gay people are incapable of forming lasting relationships. It seems that, in parallel with the ministry of *Exodus*, God had provided an alternative for those who dared simply to believe the Gospel. Unsurprisingly we met a great many ex-*Exodus* people who were also very grateful for Ralph Blair's work. Indeed, the first EC conference we attended had a strange feeling of déjà-vu for us; it felt so like an *Exodus* conference in some ways. We gradually discovered that of course most of the organisers had been *Exodus* members and leaders in the past.

20.   Caught Off Balance

Have you ever had the experience of trying to walk down an immobile escalator? This is not an unusual occurrence on London Underground. It can feel very disconcerting trying to walk down a staircase that should be moving. One feels strangely caught off balance.

As we become accustomed to using escalators, our brains adjust so that we learn how to maintain our balance whilst travelling on a moving object without having to think about it. This learned ability becomes fixed so that when we step onto a stationary escalator, the mind does not adjust easily.

We experience something similar when God calls us to reconsider a doctrine which previously had a certain popularly accepted interpretation. The sensation is disorientating and we don't find it at all pleasant. The disciples faced this kind of challenge a number of times when listening to Jesus' teaching. A striking example occurs in John's Gospel. Jesus could hardly have chosen a more offensive way of proclaiming a new doctrine than this. *Whoever eats my flesh and drinks my blood has eternal life, and I will raise him up at the last day. For my flesh is real food and my blood is real drink. Whoever eats my flesh and drinks my blood remains in me, and I in him."* (John 6:54-56)

This was so difficult to hear that many of Jesus' disciples turned back and no longer followed him (v 66). Yet when Jesus asked his closest disciples if they wanted to leave too, Simon Peter replied, *Lord to whom shall we go? You have the words of eternal life.* (v68). Having been a committed Christian for over forty years, if I'd not had a personal relationship with Jesus Christ to reassure me and guide me through life's testing challenges, I might have walked away too.

We find it easy to accept Jesus' words about eating his flesh and drinking his blood because we know the rest of the story. Jesus' disciples did not. They could not say, 'Ah, of course, I can see where this is going'. It usually takes us a long time to accept something completely new, especially when it seems at first sight to be something entirely different, perhaps even completely opposite, to what we have always been taught.

I have often wondered why Jesus provoked his disciples in this way. His approach was hardly likely to win friends and influence people. But I've noticed that one of the ways Jesus sifted his followers was by provoking the disbelief of those whose commitment was conditional upon him fitting in with the doctrines they were accustomed to.

Aware that his disciples were grumbling about this, Jesus said to them, 'Does this offend you? What if you see the Son of Man ascend to where he was before! The Spirit gives life; the flesh counts for nothing. The words I have spoken to you are spirit and they are life. Yet there are some of you who do not believe.' For Jesus had known from the beginning which of them did not believe and who would betray him. He went on to say, 'This is why I told you that no-one can come to me unless the Father has enabled him.' From this time many of his disciples turned back and no longer followed him. (John 6:61-66)

Whenever our certainties about the will of God are challenged, we inevitably experience a struggle to adjust — the stationery escalator syndrome. In recent times many gay Christians have found the confidence to speak openly about their sexual orientation in their churches. Gay Christian leaders have come out and every denomination has been disturbed by the challenge this poses.

History demonstrates that when the church is rocked by huge controversy, the response God is usually calling for is repentance. We are being asked to abandon traditional ways of operating at the expense of other people. There are often power and control issues to recognise and repent of. When we realise this we can start to respond appropriately to the needs of our own day in the way Christ did two thousand years ago. Repentance is, of course, a gift to be received from God, as Paul explains. *Do you show contempt for the riches of his kindness, tolerance and patience, not realising that God's kindness leads you towards repentance?"* (Romans 2:4) The Gospels clearly reveal Christ's acceptance of and love for every group that was routinely rejected in his day, whether they were lepers, tax collectors or women of dubious moral character.[22] Being right is not the point; being good, honest and truthful, with personal integrity, is. *Live as children of the light, for the fruit of the light consists in all goodness, righteousness and truth.* (Ephesians 5:8-9)

21.   Take up your Cross

Steve Shaw poignantly describes the inner torment of Christians who find that they are gay. *Discovering I was gay was like discovering that I was that person my mother had always warned me about.*[23] He goes on to observe that *the pressure of social, moral and religious taboos against gay sexuality is so immense that it can create the most dreadful shadow behaviour.* This has certainly been the experience of the majority of gay Christians that I know.

The world we live in brings challenges enough without us forever feeling, at a pathological level, that we are our own worst enemies. Of course we will always have a degree of struggle between our own sinful ego and the lordship of Christ. But once you have experienced a glimpse of what Jesus Christ is truly like, the love in your heart for the Lord is such that your ego does not stand much chance in opposition in the long run. The ways of the world tend to lose their compelling appeal when you have found the *treasure in the field* (Matthew 13:44, Luke 12:34).

As we learn to live in Christ, the *peace that the world cannot give* (John 14:27) and the hope and joy that Christ gives to all who truly turn to him, are evidence that our lives are in the process of redemption. Christ laid down his life to make this possible. If we are in constant inner conflict, we have surely missed something essential about the Good News. The great joy that the Gospel brings to the repentant sinner is the assurance of God's love and of God's commitment to complete the work of our redemption as we follow him. God promises peace in that assurance to everyone who walks by faith in Christ. As Paul writes, *May the God of hope fill you with all joy and peace as you trust in him, so that you may overflow with hope by the power of the Holy Spirit.* (Romans 15:13)

I have learned that Jesus' command to *take up our cross* (Matthew 10:38-39) is fundamentally a challenge to egotistical posturing, calling us to repent of the foolish agendas that we often promote in order to exercise control over our own lives and the lives of others. Whilst undeniably the Christian life may involve intense suffering at times, his challenge has little if anything to do with the need to suffer purely for the sake of it. Such a discipline is often imposed by the kind of religion that never succeeds in making anyone truly good. As Paul points out:

Since you died with Christ to the basic principles of this world, why, as though you still belonged to it, do you submit to its rules: 'Do not handle! Do not taste! Do not touch!'? These are all destined to perish with use, because they are based on human commands and teachings. Such regulations indeed have an appearance of wisdom, with their self-imposed worship, their false humility and their harsh treatment of the body, but they lack any value in restraining sensual indulgence. (Col. 2:20-23)

Some years ago, I accompanied one of our *Courage* members on a visit to see his pastor. His opening question was, 'Whatever is it that is so terrible about making love to another man that I must spend the rest of my life alone and deny myself the possibility of a loving relationship' The pastor shrugged his shoulders and replied, 'Well, I don't make the rules. It is God you must ask about this.'

The fear-based argument that we must deny ourselves intimate companionship lest it lead to sexual sin is spurious. To expect people to suffer loneliness and isolation, as if there was something virtuous in self-denial for its own sake, is heartless, not biblical. If God wishes to call us to such self-sacrifice, might we not expect to have a sense of personal conviction about it? Why would God send such a message to us through church leaders who consistently refuse to listen to our experience? They are seldom disposed to change their viewpoint if to do so would threaten their position. It is not just a question of maintaining power. Even the humblest of pastors need an income. They are understandably afraid of alienating the congregations who pay their salaries, especially if they have families to provide for.

Jesus challenged us to be child-like in our faith, confident in the Father and assured by his promise that *the Holy Spirit will lead you into all truth* (John 16:12,13). With that child-like faith, many gay Christians have found the confidence to pursue a same-sex partnership.

22.   The Gospel Undermined

Today there is open debate about the experience of gay Christians and this has challenged the fundamental convictions that many people hold about sexuality, marriage and family life in its traditional form. The worry for many Christians leaders is that if same-sex partnerships are accepted, how will we teach young people in an immoral age if rules assumed to be biblical are not upheld? Where will we find any credible authority for maintaining those essential rules of restraint? Teaching young people a sense of personal moral responsibility would not be enough, it is feared, and would certainly not control testosterone-driven young men. Shame is always a much more effective brake.

Understandably, perhaps, many pastors still default to an insistence on applying the rules indiscriminately, and remain indifferent to the suffering this causes. Only when we are really motivated to uncover the reasons for our traditions are we likely to put in the hard work needed to find a biblically credible and creative way forward. Undoubtedly the process stirs up huge controversy and those who embark upon such a risky enterprise pay dearly in loss of reputation and income. Yet failure to do the work is short-sighted. Blocking gay Christians by demanding unquestioning obedience without discussing our experience has got the church nowhere — except deep into the mire of controversy.

It is tragic but unsurprising that the church has become a laughing stock in today's world. Ordinary people just cannot understand why Christians seem to have such a voyeuristic obsession with sex. We are created to be sexual beings and we must learn to handle this in a healthy way. How much better it would be for the church to have a reputation for caring for the poor, the under-privileged and disenfranchised, as Jesus did. Christians have become infamous in our generation for expelling their lesbian and gay members, unwilling even to consider the possibility that some of us are born that way and are naturally going to desire a partner of the same-sex. Thus the credibility of the Gospel undermined.

When priests and bishops go out of their way to prevent gay Christians from finding a way forward for their lives, freed from the damaging effects of prejudice, they are practising persecution fuelled by ignorance. To fail in our moral responsibility in this way is to act like the hired hand, not like the true shepherd (John 10:12). Jesus' own example was to be a good shepherd who laid down his life for his sheep, and in so doing laid down his reputation too:

I am the good shepherd; I know my sheep and my sheep know me — just as the Father knows me and I know the Father — and I lay down my life for the sheep. I have other sheep that are not of this sheep pen. I must bring them also. They too will listen to my voice, and there shall be one flock and one shepherd. (John 10:14-16)

Nobody chooses to be gay. We discover this to be part of who we are as we grow up. There are some people who discover their homosexuality later in life, perhaps after committing to marriage. If there were truly any choice in the matter, we would surely all choose to be heterosexual. Even the appearance of being heterosexual makes life easier, and integration into church and society is less problematic. It is only later that many of us come to be comfortable and confident as gay people.

In a superb exposition of the Book of Job, entitled *Suffering and Mystery* [18] Roy Clements considers the reasons for the stand-off between Job and the comforters who attempted to make sense of his trials from their traditional perspective. Job found this tremendously frustrating because, as Clements observes, *Job's theological position on suffering changed as a result of his personal experience of it.* This sometimes happens, and helps to explain why the theological view of gay Christians can change, as a result of our suffering.

Our priests and bishops would do well to heed Jesus' words in Matthew 9:13; 12:7 (referring to Hosea 6:6): *If you had known what these words mean, 'I desire mercy not sacrifice', you would not have condemned the innocent.*

23. The Power of Prejudice

Many Christian leaders dismiss all gay people as subversives — rebels against God, and like tares in a field of wheat, sown by an enemy — to be separated out and burned on the day of judgement (Matthew 13). With that mindset, some then set out to rubbish the testimony of gay Christians on the basis of statistics about levels of promiscuity and the spread of HIV in a decadent society. But this strategy backfires to demonstrate its own absurdity.

A cynic could easily quote the figures for marital breakdown and cite the tragically high divorce rate to make a case against heterosexual marriage. Few people would listen, because we all know that a marriage stands or falls on whether or not a husband and wife love one another and work at their relationship day by day. No marriage is nourished merely by sticking to the rules. I have seen marriages fail disastrously when a husband or wife has held to a legalistic attitude without love.

Moreover, it is ludicrous to suggest that marriage could be undermined by gay Christians entering into civil partnerships. Those who propose this absurd notion, need to explain what aspect of love, commitment and faithfulness between gay people is it that undermines heterosexual marriage? We all remain unshaken in our belief that marriage is a God-given covenant and sacrosanct. Why else do churches offer so much in terms of marriage preparation classes and marriage enrichment courses? We believe that marriage is good and can work well, in spite of the challenges.

Yet when you come from a background of conservative evangelical teaching as I do, it can be very tempting to adopt a cynic's position to same-sex relationships. You research the subject, select the worst possible examples of gay conduct and then quote your findings as if they were a universal statement of fact. Why does our sense of logic not recognise that the same tactics can be used to discredit or support anything? The person who digs out statistics simply to discredit those they disagree with cannot expect to be taken seriously by anyone who values the truth. But it is clearly unnerving to feel our comfortable theological rug pulled from under our feet.

When the foundations are being destroyed, what can the righteous do?
The Lord is in his holy temple; the Lord is on his heavenly throne.
He observes everyone on earth; his eyes examine them. (Psalm 11:3-4 TNIV)

In charismatic Christian circles especially, it can be so tempting to see life in terms of a great cosmic battle between good and evil, in which the devil nearly wins the day, though we are assured that in the end, God and his legions of angels will win through somehow. Spiritual battle there may be, yet the Bible really gives no credence to such a Hollywood view of cosmic battle; God is always sovereign and is never compromised at all by the sinfulness of man or the wiles of the devil. This comes out so clearly in the Book of Job where Satan even has to ask God's permission to test him.

Another common fear comes from the belief that if people listen to us, they might be deceived themselves. So as a shield against the possibility of being taken in, they vigorously maintain, 'We want to know where we stand. We want to proclaim our position, as men and women of conviction. We want you to know that we are the ones who have the truth. We are the ones who are in the Kingdom of God. And we must warn those dissenters that they are the ones who will be cast out'.

When we allow fear to reign, if we believe that Satan is winning and the 'gay agenda' is part of his diabolical strategy – we are easily tempted to cling to a superficial interpretation of certain bible texts to maintain a position, rather than holding to a quiet reliance on the Spirit of God to lead us through the theological minefields we encounter. A well-known preacher once quizzically posed the question, 'Why is it that educated and intelligent Christians can be Members of Parliament, directors of big businesses and manage all kinds of huge responsibilities, yet when they come to church on Sunday, they unscrew their heads and leave them under their seats?'

Let us take a moment to remind ourselves of the basis of the New Covenant, as explained by the writer to the Hebrews: *But in fact the ministry Jesus has received is as superior to theirs as the covenant of which he is mediator is superior to the old one, since the new covenant is established on better promises. For if there had been nothing wrong with that first covenant, no place would have been sought for another. But God found fault with the people and said: 'The days are coming, declares the Lord, when I will make a new covenant with the house of Israel and with the house of Judah. It will not be like the covenant I made with their ancestors . . . This is the covenant I will make with the house of Israel after that time, declares the Lord. I will put my laws in their minds and write them on their hearts. I will be their God, and they will be my people. No longer will they teach their neighbours, or say to one another, 'Know the Lord,' because they will all know me, from the least of them to the greatest. For I will forgive their wickedness and will remember their sins no more. By calling this covenant 'new', he has made the first one obsolete; and what is obsolete and outdated will soon disappear.* (Hebrews 8:6-13 TNIV)

From this we see that, according to the new covenant mediated by Jesus Christ, we may have confidence in what the Holy Spirit reveals to a believer — whether gay or straight — when we have sought God with complete sincerity and are in agreement with two or more of our brethren (Matthew 18:19–20). We may have confidence because God has promised to put his laws in our hearts and write them in our minds. Above all, our relationship with God has been made possible through all that Christ has done for us. Therefore, guidance for our spiritual journey comes through faith, reason, study of the scriptures and personal experience of Holy Spirit's teaching within the community of the church.

However grateful we may be for fine theologians and visionary prophetic leaders, none of us is ultimately dependent upon them either for our salvation or for guidance as to how we should live — although I would be the first to recognise that their help along the way can be invaluable. As we mature in our faith, God does not want us to be overly dependent on the teaching of others for too long, however erudite they may be, lest we put our faith in sinners and not God.

Part of the problem is that we have for generations been accustomed to being governed by laws founded on what we have understood to be Christian principles. To a significant degree, the church has played an authoritative role in setting standards. However, in the last century the whole world has been through staggering changes, and everything, including the institutions of marriage and family life, has been challenged to the core. Nobody likes the feeling of being robbed of a position of authority. Church leaders are no exception. Jesus' example of utter humility and dedication to service (Philippians 2) is a tough act to follow, even for those of us who've been Christians for a very long time.

Our fear of change may be understandable, but we must all still agree that the Lord is sovereign and God is the one who shakes the foundations of the earth. If Jesus is still Lord and the builder of his church, we need not be worried. As Job observed, after all he had suffered, *God's plans can never be thwarted.* (Job 42:2).

Even so, it is always important to stay in close fellowship with other Christians. Their companionship on our pilgrimage is vital. Gay Christians soon feel bereft when marginalised or driven out of fellowship. Everyone is vulnerable if completely alone on their Christian walk. It is small wonder that when gay Christians have been pushed out of church, they seek the company of other gay people who have no faith. And gay people in our society generally feel pretty hostile to the church—for understandable reasons, having always been treated as pariahs and criminals in the past.

When we regarded as beyond the pale, the road away from faith can be a short one. In such circumstances some gay Christians may indeed descend into promiscuous behaviour which they would not have contemplated if they could have remained in a supportive spiritual environment.

The reason people have such difficulty in accepting gay people is surely more emotional than theological. When a homophobic father discovers that his greatly loved son or daughter is gay, he may react badly at first. But as he sees that his child does not fit the stereotype he'd always had in his mind, he begins to understand that perhaps he has been wrong. Realising that he could lose the one he greatly loves if he does not change his mind, he is gradually able to see the issues differently and come to a place of acceptance. A once incontrovertible theological position begins to seem less so.

24.   Evangelical Foundations

It's helpful to remind ourselves at this point of a very great irony. In the evangelical Protestant tradition, we challenge everybody to turn to Christ and develop a personal relationship with our heavenly Father. However did we forget the historic Reformation, that so undermined the controlling authority of the established church in the sixteenth century, releasing so many Christians from corrupt and oppressive teaching? The Reformation was founded on the same Gospel principles that in time will surely release gay people from the corrosive influence of homophobia in the church today.

The central importance of the scriptures is a core value of the evangelical church, to be sure. But in studying the scriptures, our emphasis must be on weighing the teaching we have been given, as commended in Acts 17:11. The Berean Jews were noted to be sincere disciples who *studied the scriptures to see if Paul's teaching was true.* Gay Christians who have been brought up as evangelicals follow the same path to Christ as their straight brothers and sisters. So when they, with sincere conviction, take a view that challenges the traditional understanding of homosexuality, then as evangelicals, if we believe in our own core values, we should give them an honest hearing.

Martin Luther's understanding that salvation comes by faith in what Christ has done for us was fundamental to the efficacy of the Reformation in the sixteenth century and remains fundamental to Christian faith today. Since we must all stand to give account before God, who among evangelical Christians dares presume that their interpretation of the Bible on a point of doctrine has greater validity because they are heterosexual? When gay people are made to run the gauntlet of opprobrium because we have had the effrontery to be open and truthful about ourselves, the judgmental attitudes of our detractors become transparent. Such attitudes are manifestly false because they are based on ignorance and prejudice without love. But *love never fails.* (1 Corinthians 13:1-3, 8 & 13).

We forget at our peril that a relationship with God is a gift, to be respected. For Jesus said, *No-one can come to me unless the Father who sent me draws him, and I will raise him up at the last day. It is written in the Prophets: 'They will all be taught by God.' Everyone who listens to the Father and learns from him comes to me.* (John 6:44-45)

From time to time we are all bound to take a view that brings us into conflict with people who understand things differently. But we should never forget that, if we adopt a posture of interpretive superiority, we not only exchange our Christ-given robe of humility for pride (1 Peter 5:5), but we challenge the very basis of the new covenant in Christ.

We have been called to serve one another, not to judge. So when a fellow Christian disagrees with a doctrine we consider sacrosanct, we must guard against the subtle temptation to insist without listening that our particular interpretation is right. In being dismissive, we are failing to respect the sanctity of a fellow believer's relationship with God. We all have to guard against the temptation to outlaw those who have a different perspective from us. Gay Christians can fall into the same trap—dismissing our opponents as mere traditionalists whose views are outdated.

My wife and I love a plaque on the wall of a friend's house that reminds us of what really matters. *We are not here to see through each other, but to see each other through.*

25.   A Longing Fulfilled

Having considered the question of same-sex partnerships and scripture in considerable depth elsewhere [24], in this book I have focussed on the pastoral imperatives that led us to change our approach.

We've seen already that in the beginning, in a perfect world, God acknowledged that man needs companionship. (Genesis 2:18) Those whom Jesus acknowledged would be unable to marry (Matthew 19) and who find lifelong celibacy unsustainable, can clearly benefit from a godly same-sex relationship. Sexual intimacy is as important for gay people as for everyone else. We saw that this was far preferable to people giving up hope and, in their despair, getting themselves into some very unhealthy situations.

Having worked in full-time ministry with gay Christians for many years, seeing the pastoral issues at first hand, I could not believe that God was indifferent to the prayers of those we worked with. He has, after all, promised to reward those who earnestly seek him (Hebrews 11:6). Nor could I believe that God just abandons his disciples to frustration and despair, condemning them forever if they pursue relationships that, according to traditional teaching, he can never accept.

In Proverbs 13:12 we read that h*ope deferred makes the heart sick, but a longing fulfilled is a tree of life.* We understood the first part of the verse only too well. Now we wanted to encounter the second. Every Christian experiences periods of struggle with sin, but for the Christian who has a constant inner battle with same-sex attraction, some resolution must be found in the end, or his hope in Christ has no meaning. Besides, such an unremitting battle is inconsistent with Paul's advice that *it is better to marry than to burn.* (1 Corinthians 7:9) Unfortunately, where gay people are concerned, the attitude has tended to be, 'Burn now, or burn later — in hell!' But this is callously inconsistent with the pastoral attitude of Jesus and Paul. Indeed, Paul's words to Timothy, in which he describes the forbidding of marriage as a doctrine of demons, are surely as applicable to the forbidding of same-sex partnerships (1 Timothy 4:3). Paul concluded his argument by saying, *For everything God created is good, and nothing is to be rejected if it is received with thanksgiving, because it is consecrated by the word of God and prayer* (1 Timothy 4:4-5) . Why should we not accept that same-sex partnerships are a gift of grace too, and give thanks to God? To us this is just common sense.

As far as we know, Jesus never married but he surely had a special place in his heart for Mary Magdalene, and he was known to have a beloved disciple (John 13:23-25; 20:2; 21:7; 21:20). As gay people, why should we not follow our Lord's example? To those who hasten to argue that Jesus was not having a gay relationship, we find ourselves responding in Jesus' words, *What is that to you?* (John 21:22).

26.   The Lens of Sexuality

No-one pours new wine into old wineskins. If he does, the new wine will burst the skins, the wine will run out and the wineskins will be ruined. No, new wine must be poured into new wineskins. And no-one, after drinking the old wine wants the new, for he says, 'The old is better.' (Luke 5:37-39 NIV)

By the year 2000, it had become clear that God was requiring of the *Courage* ministry a marked change of attitude, outlook and policy. But contemplating this new perspective created significant tensions and raised some hugely important questions for us. And since our churches could not accept the direction in which we were going, we had to create a fellowship of our own.

We took comfort from Jesus' words about new and old wineskins. For us, the new wine was the life-giving good news that committed, faithful same-sex partnerships are on God's agenda. Tragically this good news for gay Christians is splitting the church. It came as no surprise that conservative evangelical churches simply accused us of capitulating to the current world view, in approving the gay lifestyle. In using the expression 'gay lifestyle', our critics were surely intending to insinuate that gay men and women are incapable of falling in love and are only interested in pursuing sex out of unbridled and deviant lust. We knew in our own hearts that this was not so. We also knew that generally speaking, heterosexual people find the idea of a same-sex relationship repugnant.   But while we could respect their differences of view, we could no longer allow our lives to be governed by homophobic or prejudiced attitudes.

It must by now be obvious that the real battleground for most straight Christian people is not a theological one at all. It is the result of being brought up in a culture that has been endemically anti-gay. Our model for relationships has always been one of heterosexual romance — affirmed in virtually every story, play or film.   Heterosexual romance has the predominant call on the hearts of most people — including those of us who are gay and have not been able to accept the truth about ourselves. We are not accustomed to anything else. When we have, built into our thinking, the belief that all same-sex activity is perverted, it is very hard to overcome the emotional and psychological reactions we have been programmed to make. This is not at all dissimilar to the reactions of white people towards people of colour, which led to the tragedy of racial prejudice and segregation for so many generations. Hopefully our societies are becoming more genuinely civilised in dealing with the abomination of racial prejudice. But we need to see that the same dynamic exists towards gay people and requires the same change in our core values. The church lags behind instead of showing the way forward as it did in previous generations, when Christians were pioneers in providing education, medical expertise and care for the poor.

The assurance that such a change of attitude can happen occurred recently at one of our bi-annual *Courage* retreats, when a straight married couple had booked in to join us. They had shown a genuine interest in our ministry. At the last moment, the wife had to respond to a family illness and could not come, so her husband came alone. Let's call him Paul. On the first evening, over dinner, Paul confessed to me that he felt really uncomfortable about being there on his own, because he was afraid that people might assume he was gay. He clearly felt the need to tell me that he found the thought of gay sex absolutely disgusting. I tried to reassure him that we had all come here to worship God and enjoy Christian fellowship, not to proposition people, whether they were gay or straight. I also suggested that it might be better not to let his imagination run away with him. 'After all,' I said to him, 'I would not spend my time thinking about you having sex with your wife. It just isn't appropriate; it's a private matter between the two of you.' His need to be thinking about gay sex at this time annoyed me. Personally I've never felt the need to conjure up in my mind what straight couples do sexually, least of all in order to vicariously experience a feeling of disgust about it.

At the end of the meal, when we were laying tables for breakfast, one of the *Courage* members made a joke on a gay theme, prompted by something quite trivial. Everyone laughed out loud except Paul, whose face went ashen. He said to me with a shudder, 'I've never been with any group before who see everything in life through the lens of their sexuality.' I found myself replying quite spontaneously, 'But it is you who see everything through the lens of our sexuality. That is why we are not allowed to preach, lead house groups, Sunday school or youth groups, or even take part in a communion service in many churches. If we admit to being gay, church people seem to see everything we do through the lens of our sexuality, and they judge us as being unfit for purpose.' 'I see what you mean,' he replied. 'I had not thought of it that way before.'

At the final session, when we were sharing what God had done for us that weekend, Paul spoke up, slowly and solemnly. 'I have to confess to you all that I am straight. My wife just could not be with us because of a family illness. I must admit that at first I felt uncomfortable being here on my own. But you have been kind enough to welcome me into your midst without prejudice. I see now that you have created a safe place for yourselves to come together and enjoy Christian fellowship – to worship, pray and study the Bible together – because the churches you come from are not safe. And now I see that the reason churches are not safe for you is, basically. . . because of people like me.' This was a profoundly moving moment for us all. We were deeply touched by his humility and kindness. But it was not until he had faced his fears and got to know us as real people that Paul's strong feelings of antipathy were diminished.

27.   Beyond Ex-Gay

Trying to maintain a credible basis for Christian ministry in the eyes of our critics and remain faithful to what we believed God was saying to us became impossible. Some of our former supporters were quick to judge and withdrew their funding because they felt our commitment to biblical standards was being compromised. Some critics argued that sin might appear to satisfy in the short term, but this was no excuse.

A turning point for those who've always regarded these matters as non-negotiable, begins when they can recognise the reality of the acutely painful dilemmas faced by gay people. Compassion tends to prompt prayer, and with prayer comes connection between Christ and suffering of people who are misunderstood. When the life-giving message of the Gospel kicks into action, the effect always brings transformation. One of the outstanding characteristics of Jesus' own ministry was the way he lived with outcasts and worked with the reality of their situations. It was not for nothing that Jesus was scoffed at for being *a friend of sinners.* (Matt 11:16-19).

We must surely understand that to sin is to fall short of the glory of God. The Good News is that, once we know our own need of God's forgiveness and receive his grace, our hope lies in what God has done for us in Christ. Our hope is never placed in what we can achieve for ourselves, as if somehow we could make ourselves sinless. Our hope is always in the redemptive work of Christ. Anything else is idolatry. It is a change of heart that God requires from us. By contrast, the attempt to change sexual orientation through healing prayer seems to have more to do with the church's requirement for conformity than anything that God requires.

It is easy for heterosexual married pastors to demand a life of celibacy as the biblical answer for homosexual people. They have little experience of the years of aching loneliness we have known. But for those in spiritual authority to continually frustrate gay people, more on account of their personal disgust at our sexuality than out of real biblical conviction, is deeply unjust. They could revise their interpretation of Scripture in relation to birth control and divorce and remarriage — in spite of the fact that birth control interferes with nature and remarriage for divorced people is categorically prohibited in Scripture from a literal reading of the texts. Theological revision on compassionate grounds could be undertaken when there was strong personal interest at stake. This may feel a suspect reason for revision but it is not in itself wrong, especially when suffering has been caused for so long by a misuse of the scriptures. A crisis situation is often the only thing that will ever motivate us to reconsider our position.

Jesus pointed out this dynamic when he rebuked people for their hypocrisy over the keeping of the Sabbath law *He said to them, 'If any of you has a sheep and it falls into a pit on the Sabbath, will you not take hold of it and lift it out? How much more valuable is a man than a sheep! Therefore it is lawful to do good on the Sabbath.'* (Matthew 12:11-12)

Reassuringly we were not alone in recognising that the time had come for reassessment. Many folk who had left our ministry in the early days returned, having made a similar journey themselves. We were able to agree together that this was the way the Lord was leading us. We had learned to accept what we could not change about ourselves, and were learning to live as gay Christians with our heads held high, knowing that we were children of God, by faith, and that God understood and is happy to bless our desire for a relationship with someone of the same sex. God clearly did not want it any other way — he had a large following of gay Christian people who had devoted the best years of their lives to the process of change, and our strategy had been a dismal failure.

Dr Roy Clements makes the following observation in his excellent article, *Why evangelicals must think again about homosexuality.* [25]

Jesus famously provided a hermeneutic tool to help his followers to negotiate their way through moral debates about Old Testament law. He identified one Levitical command as the key to understanding the rationale behind all the others: *Love your neighbour as yourself* (Mark 12:31; Matthew 22:39-40 —quoting Leviticus 19:18). Paul, too, affirms the same insight (Romans 13:9-10 and Galatians 5:14). This suggests that, when trying to determine why an Old Testament law was given and what its relevance is to a modern Christian, two vital questions must be asked:

> What harm to my neighbour was this command intended to prevent?
> What good to my neighbour was this command intended to promote?

Indeed, similar enquiry into the original purpose of law underlies the science of jurisprudence generally. The radical consequences which resulted from Jesus looking at the Sabbath in this way are clear in the Gospels. He flagrantly disregarded the onerous rabbinical interpretations of what Sabbath observance required, on the grounds that the institution was intended to be a blessing not a burden (Mark 2:27). The application of the same interpretive principles to Leviticus 18:21 and 19:4 might similarly lead to more compassionate conclusions regarding homosexuality. It is certainly very difficult to see in what way a total ban on all expressions of homoerotic affection should be demanded as a rational expression of neighbour love.

In 2007 Christine Bakke and Peterson Toscano took an important initiative by opening a website to encourage people who have survived the 'ex-gay' movement to meet together.[26] Joining with *Soulforce*[27] they organised a special *Ex-Gay Survivors Conference* [28] in Irvine, California to coincide with the *Exodus* North America conference. Before the conference, I was able to join Michael Busee, one of the original founders of *Exodus,* and Darlene

Bogle, whom I had known in my days with *Love in Action*. We had the opportunity to make a public well-publicised apology to all gay people for our involvement in the 'ex-gay' movement. [29] This was an important moment: we were able to declare publicly that the 'ex-gay' ethos is damaging and that the promises of the 'ex-gay' movement are, at best misleading, but overall quite wrong in the agenda they propose, in the light of experience. The one redeeming thing that can be said for the 'ex-gay' movement is that it provides a half-way house for people coming out of anti-gay churches — for those people whose backgrounds would not have allowed them to accept a gay-affirming ethos straight away.

28.   Biblical Pragmatism

The Bible is full of examples of God's pragmatism in his dealings with sinful mankind. God's toleration of polygamy and concubinage (2 Samuel 5:13; 1 Kings 11:3) comes to mind, as does his toleration of divorce (Deuteronomy 24:1); his toleration of slavery and the slaughter on a vast scale of Israel's enemies (1 Chronicles 22:8).

Biblical law was given at a time when people saw nothing wrong in a man having many wives. We do not accept this today. With a modern view of the true value of women, we believe that polygamy is contrary to God's creation of men and women as equals. Why then did the Bible not forbid it unequivocally? How was it that Moses dared to permit divorce when it is clear from Jesus' teaching that God was always against it? (Matthew 19:8-9) Jesus explained that *Moses* allowed this *because of the hardness of men's hearts*, suggesting that those in spiritual leadership do have discretion in determining right practice for the Christian community (Matthew 16:18-20).

The good news is that mercy and compassion underline the ministry of Jesus. His severest criticism was reserved for leaders who failed to show these qualities. *Woe to you, teachers of the law and Pharisees, you hypocrites! You shut the kingdom of heaven in people's faces. You yourselves do not enter, nor will you let those enter who are trying to.* (Matthew 23:13 TNIV)

Also, appropriately in view of our subject, Jesus observed that, *the teachers of the law and the Pharisees sit in Moses' seat. So you must obey them and do everything they tell you. But do not do what they do, for they do not practise what they preach. They tie up heavy loads and put them on men's shoulders, but they themselves are not willing to lift a finger to move them.'* (Matthew 23:2-4)

In his letter to the Romans, Paul described a people under God's judgement because they had turned their backs on God, and were abandoned to their own agendas, *women exchanging natural relations* and men *becoming inflamed with lust for one another* (Romans 1:26-27). It is totally inappropriate to include in that judgement gay people who have whole-heartedly sought God over many years.

Moses and Paul both sought God for themselves and their people — and would surely not expect us to uncritically impose biblical statutes drawn up for a bygone age today. They sought God for the circumstances they faced in their day. They would hardly expect us to do less.

An interesting illustration of God's priorities in dealing with sexual immorality can be found in the story of David and Bathsheba. In 2 Samuel 12, we see that King David — the man after God's own heart — could have several wives and not provoke God's judgement. But when he took another man's wife, God did not merely send the prophet Nathan to accuse David of adultery, as contemporary pastors might. Rather, God's judgement was given because David — who already had all the wives he wanted and could have asked for more — had taken *the ewe lamb that belonged to a poor man* (2 Samuel 12:1-10). The poignant illustration that Nathan used to convict David graphically illustrates the contrast between God's anger and grief at the violation of Uriah and Bathsheba's marriage, and the tendency of modern pastors to rush to puritanical judgement over genital acts.

Similarly, in 1 Corinthians 5, Paul condemned the man who had taken his father's wife. The judgement was not made merely on the grounds that he had sex with another woman. It was the fact that the man had publicly dishonoured his father that prompted Paul's indignation (see Leviticus 18:8). We must remember that Paul's world was a patriarchal one in which it was considered terrible to dishonour a man, whereas a woman could simply be used because she had minimal rights. My point is that both stories reveal God's concern for the well-being of vulnerable people's; clearly this is what takes priority in God's heart. Jesus died for people, not merely for principles. His comments on the Sabbath law make that quite clear. He gave his life that we might be reconciled to the Father, not that moral standards might be raised.

The whole question of what constitutes sexual immorality requires a paper in itself. Suffice to say that, throughout scripture, the morality or otherwise of sexual behaviour is not determined by the legitimacy of certain kinds of genital contact. The Bible never defines sexual behaviour in these terms. Yet tragically the arguments against homosexual practice are often reduced to this level. But even at this level there is a lesson to be learned. When Abraham instructed his chief servant to *put your hand under my thigh and swear*, he was actually asking the man to put his hand on his master's testicles in order to swear an oath — a common practice in those times. (Genesis 24:2) A man's testicles were considered sacred — a source of life — and the idea of placing one's hand there to swear an oath is a forerunner of our modern courtroom practice that requires a person to place their hand on the Bible and swear to tell the truth in speaking or giving evidence. The ancient practice would be far too culturally anachronistic to be considered appropriate today; anyone trying it would very likely be arrested and charged with sexual harassment. My point is simply that our perceptions of what is appropriate or inappropriate are so culturally conditioned that they cannot be an objective a test of right and wrong in the way we like to claim.

Relationship is the key issue — relationship between God and his people, between a man and a woman in marriage, and between any one of us and our neighbour. God's laws clearly reflect the importance us fulfilling our responsibilities towards one another. The morally upright man, even with several wives, protects and provides for them and for his children. The immoral man thinks only of his pleasure, regardless of the cost to others.

People who are serious about their moral responsibilities before God do not take the easy way out, resorting to proof texts. Failure to do so is to act with moral cowardice. Our relationship with God is the most challenging relationship of all. We can stand with integrity before God only if we are prepared to engage with the challenges of our day. A few years ago I believed that God forbade homosexual relationships and I would have argued then that our moral responsibility lay in being obedient to that prohibition. When I realised the deeply negative effects of applying that prohibition to those seeking my pastoral care, I was bound to do what Jesus always did and give the casting vote to compassion.

29.   Authority to Decide

Christ has given us the authority to help gay Christians. This seems to have been conveniently overlooked by the church. In Matthew 16:17-19 and 18:18-20, Jesus gave authority to the Christian community to bind or loose — forbid or permit — certain things they agreed on before God. According to David H. Stern in his *Introduction to the Jewish Bible*, Jews would have understood this to mean that Jesus gave authority to his disciples to decide what practices should be followed by the community, transferring this power from the rabbis to his own disciples. The requirement was simply that two or three, gathered together in Jesus' name, should come to agreement in prayer together. We see an example of the outworking of this at the Council of Jerusalem when the apostles and elders met to decide what instructions should be given to the new Gentile believers (Acts 15:19-20). They concluded by commending two important principles — that new believers should shun idolatry and sexual immorality. These guiding principles remain as important as ever.

So the truth is that the church today does have the biblical authority to release gay Christians to form committed same-sex partnerships. Failure to do so, I believe, indicates a meanness of spirit among church leaders which has nothing to do with the pursuit of holiness and has more to do with unwillingness to engage with a subject that does not interest them, or is not expedient for them. Pleading 'biblical principles' sanitises their indifference.

The Bible is surely given by God so that we may begin to develop an understanding of truths and divine mysteries that would otherwise be completely beyond us. Without the scriptures, our understanding could never rise above the level of speculation. Even with biblical revelation, how much can any of us really understand about the nature of heaven and hell or reconciliation with a God whose awesome glory is beyond our imagination? To begin to understand the great mysteries of God and of our relationship with him, we have no choice but to study and endeavour to interpret biblical metaphor. Much of our understanding is naturally informed by scholars and Bible teachers — some of whom are more than happy to do all the thinking for us if we were not careful. It is always tempting to let others do the work of seeking God on our behalf. When we have grown up to interpret doctrine according to one particular paradigm, we inevitably tend to develop a controlling metaphor through which we understand everything. We need to recognise this if we are to have a humble attitude to our own ability truly to understand the mind of God.

Our controlling metaphors about marriage and sexual relationships are naturally governed by our experience and influenced by the Church's traditional teaching. None of us can avoid this. But when insistence upon doing things in a certain traditional way causes serious distress to a group of our fellow believers, it behoves us all to consider that we could be mistaken. Biblical prohibitions of sexual immorality are all set in the context of selfish exploitation and abuse of others for personal gratification. None of the hundreds of gay Christians I have met is arguing that it would be acceptable to live that way.   To those who claim that 'healing from homosexuality' is possible, we have to say that after more than ten years of working in 'ex-gay' ministry, we cannot with integrity uphold a message that God plainly does not support. The evidence is that it just does not work. Give them five years and their apparent change breaks down. Even ministry leaders get caught out in porn stores or gay bars, as the well-publicised story of *Exodus* poster boy John Paulk illustrated so startlingly. [30]

This is not a form of special pleading [18]. We do not dismiss traditional beliefs as if they were of no consequence. However, we have spent the best years of our lives trying to see ourselves by the light of the traditional controlling metaphor, and we have found it to be seriously wanting. The charge of special pleading could be applied more appropriately to those who want to see their own traditions confirmed regardless of the evidence. When they exclude a whole group of God-fearing people from the Kingdom of Heaven, it is not out of concern for the Gospel.

30.   Two Trees in the Garden

In his helpful book *There were Two Trees in the Garden*, Rick Joyner reminds us of the two trees in the Garden of Eden — the tree of life and the tree of knowledge of good and evil. The fruit of the latter was, as we all know, strictly forbidden. Ironically, the debate over homosexuality seldom rises above arguments over our understanding of good and evil. If we were to focus on Christ — the tree of life — then even if we cannot agree, we might find it easier to accept differing views. We would be honouring Christ as the head of the church above our own opinion of what is right and wrong.

We obviously find the fruit of the tree of knowledge of good and evil to be intoxicating. We are all so tempted to go on eating it — greedily. Perhaps this is because it so readily offers us the transitory power of being right — enabling us to pass judgement on those we believe are wrong. But this is not the way of the Holy Spirit who empowers us to seek reconciliation with God and our fellow human beings.

In Christ, the fruit of the tree of life has become available to us again. The gift of his life for our sake, given through the greatest suffering and personal sacrifice, must surely become our focus. When we understand this, our preoccupation with the rights and wrongs of homosexuality can be recognised as a red herring. It has allowed heterosexual people to take on the role of judge and has taken away the right that all people have — gay and straight — to seek and know God for themselves. The mandate Jesus gave to the church — to preach the Good News to all people — must always be our focus. Potential schism over homosexuality is a loud wake-up call to the church in our generation. We have forsaken the gospel, as demands for people to accept a traditional doctrinal viewpoint on homosexuality has become a *shibboleth* [31] for acceptance in churches, especially in leadership.

It is ironic that people who find homosexuality hard to accept, are so quick to quote Romans 1:25, against us, telling us that we have *exchanged the truth of God for a lie*. In fact something very different and dangerous happened. Instead, many of us exchanged the truth about *ourselves* for a lie, trying to conform to a narrow *perception* of what the Bible demands. Focussing on right doctrine and warning against wrong doctrine is to feed on forbidden fruit. So we feed from the tree of knowledge of good and evil and die, instead of finding our nourishment from the tree of life, in Jesus Christ.

Increasingly I have seen that living to get it right for God is utterly self-centred and self-righteous. It inoculates people against living a life of faith instead of trusting in the living God who loves us and dwells amongst us. I also see that commitment to righteousness and truth, as understood by the more fundamentalist Christian groups these days, has to do with imposing human agendas that are themselves profoundly sinful. They fall short of the righteousness of God, because they control people rather than giving them life. If instead, we listen to the voice of Jesus, he gently and warmly invites us to share with him a new way of living. We come to appreciate the values which express the character of the God who created us, who loves us, who walks with us and invites us to do something creative with our lives.

Hard though it is for some to accept, I've learned from the example of many gay Christian friends that a life of mutual love with a partner of the same-sex can be profoundly creative. Loving relationships always have that great potential because they take our eyes off ourselves and encourage nurture and unselfish caring for others, as every good marriage demonstrates. Sexuality — wrongly used — leads to the abuse of others, gay or straight.

The only appropriate repentance for denying the simple truth about my sexuality and for allowing myself to be driven by fear into pursuing bogus religious purity is to speak out about it. I feel sorrow and shame for having colluded with the misguided religious right. May Christ have mercy on me.

I have sometimes been asked by members of shocked congregations, what we have done to make reparation for the damage we did to the people who sought our help? It is important to remember that if we had not pursued a conservative approach, none of the people who were looking for help from an evangelical perspective would have joined us. They all came from churches with the same anti-gay ethos. We raised their hopes for the way out they were seeking. Had we affirmed homosexuality, they would have rejected us as liberal heretics. The journey of discovering that we had been wrong was one that everybody who participated in our ministry needed to go on. Without it, we would forever have wondered what might have been if only we had tried a little harder and for a little longer. The majority from the early days of *Courage* have come along with this change of approach at their own pace. A few still hold a conservative viewpoint and reject us.

The only reparation we can make today is to teach the truth as we have learned it, and pray that those men and women still entrenched in a rigidly fundamentalist outlook, will learn from our experience. This is an ongoing journey and we do not know all the answers. But I believe it is fair to say, in our own defence, that we always believed, taught and endeavoured to demonstrate that God is gracious and loving, full of compassion and mercy. We believed it was important to be uncompromising, but we were gracious in our approach, not domineering or abusive in our attitudes.

James Alison pursues these themes further in a way I find poetic and profound, and gives me some insight into how I need to move on:
It is part of the mercy of the Catholic faith that those of us who are infected by spiritual haughtiness find ourselves being lowered slowly and gently into the mud, the slime, of being one of ordinary humanity, and learning that it is this ordinary humanity which is loved as it is. If there are to be any diamonds, they will be found amidst the clay, and as the outworking of the pressures in the clay, not perched on high, on stalks, trying to avoid being infected by so much common carbon.[3][2]

However fallen the human race may be, we are all made in the image of God. When we seek to understand the truth with honesty and integrity, we may rightly have the confidence that God will speak to us. Otherwise the Christian life takes us no further than studying a book to get instructions-that-must-be-obeyed, rather than giving us a relationship with the living God, who dwells amongst us and draws us to himself.

It is a great pity that so few clergy in the days of my childhood saw the need to teach the scriptures or give churchgoers any informed understanding of what the Christian faith is all about. Perhaps that was because generations of established Anglicanism in this country made church leaders complacent. But that has changed greatly in my lifetime as increasing secularism has drawn people away from the church. Today, the Anglican Church leads the way in offering opportunities to learn the basics of the faith.

These are exciting times for the church, not because charismatic preachers are promising miracles and revival around the corner, but because disillusionment with the hype has forced many sincere Christians to look again at the scriptures and seek God afresh. A wealth of new books full of inspiration and hope is emerging. My most recent discovery has been a book by Peter Rollins from Northern Ireland who has written *How (Not) to Speak of God.* [33] Part one is entitled *Heretical Orthodoxy: from right belief to believing in the right way.* Peter Rollins explores how,

. . .orthodoxy is no longer (mis)understood as the opposite of heresy but rather is understood as a term that signals a way of being in the world rather than a means of believing things about the world. . . This approach opens up a Christian thinking that profoundly challenges some of the most basic ideas found in the contemporary Church. It is an approach which emphasises the priority of love: not as something which stands opposed to the knowledge of God, but, more radically still, *as* knowledge of God. To love is to know God precisely because God is love." "Orthodoxy as right belief will cost us little; indeed it will allow us to sit back with our Pharisaic doctrines, guarding the 'truth' with the purity of our interpretations. But orthodoxy, as believing in the right way, as bringing love to the world around us and within us . . . That will cost us everything. For to live by that sword, as we all know, is to die by it.

31. The Way Forward

We have used Romans 1 to condemn homosexuality but have been blind to Paul's underlying message — that in recognising the truth about ourselves we would become free to discover the appropriate way to live as gay Christians. How could we ever come to know the truth about God, when we refused to accept the truth about ourselves? Christians who doubted the truth about themselves just ended up *worshipping and serving created things rather than the Creator,* the created things in this case being conservative Christian opinion, uninformed by real life experience — with catastrophic results.

We are all members of one body, and when one member suffers, all suffer (1 Corinthians 12:26). Peter wrote, *Above all love one another deeply, because love covers over a multitude of sins.* (1 Peter 4:8). I know of no better method for addressing these issues.

As gay Christians who have grappled with these difficult issues and paid a heavy price for seeking to live with integrity, we have found our hope in Christ alone. Through our relationship with Jesus Christ, we have found peace with ourselves and a sense of God's acceptance of committed same-sex partnerships. We realised that expressing our convictions would cost us our reputation and that we would lose credibility with most of our fellow evangelical Christians. Some of us have felt a bit like those early disciples who, on hearing Jesus' radical and unpalatable message about eating his flesh and drinking his blood, wanted to leave. But we have had to say, along with the few who stayed with Jesus, *Lord, to whom shall we go? You have the words of eternal life.* (John 6:68)

We are not arguing that the Bible takes a soft, tolerant stance that erodes important moral principles; nor are we saying that because we are all under grace now, anything goes. However, allowance is made in the Bible for us to determine truth and its application under the guidance of the Holy Spirit. In Romans 14, Paul gives a discourse on accepting those whose faith is weak, warning us not to quarrel over debatable matters. On the question of whether or not it was acceptable to eat meat offered to idols, Paul makes it clear that there is scope for different views, according to conscience. [34]

On this basis, let us find our peace in God and encourage one another in the faith, trusting at all times in the love and sovereignty of our Lord and Saviour Jesus Christ, and not in our own understanding. The message of forgiveness and redemption through the grace of God is the very essence of the Good News of Jesus Christ.

We may have imagined that we knew what the Bible had to say on sexual matters. But the polarisation over homosexuality has only shown us how little we know. We must broaden our outlook or schism is certain. Today, as at the beginning, fruit gathered from the tree of knowledge of good and evil is toxic stuff. To challenge our assumptions and push us out of our comfort zones, God has had to stop the escalator for a while to carry out essential maintenance and repairs to the church's attitude. We are bound to feel off-balance while the rebuilding work is underway.

Jesus said, *I will build my church and the gates of hell shall not prevail against it.* (Matthew 16:18 KJV). If we could agree together to trust Jesus' promise and let him get on and build his church, we would not be facing schism now.

Epilogue: I Sang to the Harp its own Song

No attack against any one person or organisation is intended in this book. If I had wanted to rubbish the ministries of those who have disowned and rubbished me, I could have found the material. But this would not be consistent with the Spirit of Christ. Because I love the Lord, and the people I have learned from and worked with over many years, I do not now wish to carp and cavil over the injustices we have suffered, or the hurt of being rejected and misunderstood. Everybody suffers in this way to some extent, and we all hurt each other, especially when we have strong convictions about core values. My heart simply longs to see Christ shine brightly through this whole debacle of the impending schism over homosexuality. We all know that arguing about it will not resolve anything. The best we can do is listen to one another, and disagree.

Ten years after founding *Courage*, I slowly began to recognise the putrefying fruit of our work. We had been rooted in traditional conservative Christian teaching but I began to realise how false much of our ethos had been. With the support and inspiration of many others, I was able to change the course of our ministry and begin to help gay people find true freedom in Christ – a freedom beyond our hopes and dreams. As I began to recognise my own internalised homophobia, I too came to find full acceptance in Christ.

Sadly, in choosing that freedom in Christ, I lost the fellowship and support of a great many good friends and fellow pilgrims. They felt I had forsaken the truth and embraced a heresy. That has been a serious and tragic loss. My hope in writing this book is that my fellow evangelical Christians will come to see that full acceptance of gay people and same-sex partnerships does not mean renouncing the lordship of Christ or forsaking the authority of scripture. I pray they will come to recognise that the gay Christian journey is as serious a commitment to Christ as any other Christian journey. I hope to see the day come when, struggling 'ex-gays' and gay Christians can work together for the healing of our whole community. We have so much experience we could share together. But unless we can see that we are all the same and until we can rise above the demarcation lines we've drawn on the ground, we will not be united in Christ.

In Christ, we gain a new perspective that enables us to cross the lines that we have previously drawn in the ground — the lines that separate women from men, black from white, sinner from saint, gay from straight. Once we allow Jesus to be our teacher, we begin to see the reality of his words, *the kingdom of heaven is at hand.* Then we can take up the honourable assignment of using those *keys to the kingdom of heaven* that Christ has given us (Matthew 16:19) to open the gates to all who would enter in. We have to leave the keys to death and Hades with Jesus. Had he not kept those for himself (Revelation 1:18) we would surely spend our time throwing one another into hell, and jumping in ourselves at times of despair.

Richard Wurmbrand is one of my greatest heroes. He was brought up as a Jew, came to Christ and then became a Lutheran Pastor in Romania before the Communist take-over in 1945. Because of his outspoken views, he spent fourteen years in Communist prisons, frequently tortured for his faith. He eventually came to the West and I was fortunate to hear him preach a number of times when he visited the UK in the 1970s and 80s. The radiant and Christ-like love that shines out of his many amazing accounts of persecuted Christians in prison, is a shining jewel whose brilliance will last forever. During the long hours of incarceration and misery, prisoners used to tell stories to pass the time. This one, for me, captures the Spirit of Christ.

We began to tell stories, and when I was asked for one, I thought of the song, and told them this old Jewish legend. King Saul of Israel brought David, the shepherd honoured for killing Goliath, to his court. David loved music, and he was delighted to see a harp of great beauty standing in the palace. Saul said, 'I paid much for that instrument, but I was deceived. It gives forth only ugly sounds.' David took it up to try, and drew from it music so exquisite that every man was moved. The harp seemed to laugh and sing and weep. King Saul asked, 'How is it that all the musicians I called brought discord from this harp, and only you could bring out music?'

David, the future king, replied, 'Before me, each man tried to play his own song on these strings. But I sang to the harp its own song. I recalled how it had been a young tree, with birds that chirped in its branches and limbs green with leaves that blossomed in the sun. I reminded it of the day when men came to cut it down; and you heard it weep under my fingers. I explained then that this is not the end. Its death as a tree meant the start of a new life in which it would glorify God, as a harp; and you heard how it rejoiced under my hands.

So, when the Messiah comes, many will try to sing on His harp their own songs, and their tunes will be harsh. We must sing on His harp His own song, the song of His life, passions, joys, sufferings, death and resurrection. Only then will the music be true. [5]

A Word From My Wife Bren

It was a calm, clear day when Jeremy and I married on 5th October 1991. We made our vows to each other in the presence of a great many family and friends, and we were also conscious that God in his Heaven witnessed our solemnity and celebration as well. We had both already known tough times: I as a woman, fighting the battle to have a place in church leadership, and Jeremy because he is gay. Neither of us knew how tough our journey together would become as we faced hostility and exclusion from group after group. It is as well that God hides the future from us. Certainly we have learnt the truth of the phrase, *Sufficient unto the day is the evil thereof.*

God is the greatest creator. Every blade of grass is different from the other. Every snowflake is different. Every human being is unique, and God works differently in and through us all. If I see God working one way in a particular situation, I quickly discover that he is operating quite differently in another, apparently parallel, set of circumstances. The thorny question of physical healing is a good example. For one person the route to healing seems to be through forgiveness. For another, healing comes instantaneously; in another, through a lengthy process and in another not at all. The only clarity I have about the question of healing is that God either does it or doesn't. There are no certainties.

Certainty is the opposite of faith. If we knew the answers to all our questions, what need would there be for faith? And if we could understand all about Almighty God then he would cease to be almighty. Our world is becoming more and more uncertain, with terrorist attacks, world poverty and war graphically splashed onto our TV screens every hour. Many of us therefore crave certainty. We cling to people who appear confident and certain. Such individuals appear to know where they are going, and we get a sense of safety and security from them. Yet God calls us to a life of faith. He will not be tied to man-made principles. If the Christian life was a series of comprehensible situations with set solutions, what need would there be for God at all?

So it is in the gay-straight world. For some gay people it is God's purpose that they have a same-sex partner. For some it seems their destiny is to remain single. For others it may be good to be married, yet for others it definitely is not. What should our response be to a mixed marriage? Jeremy is a gay, I am not. I tend not to call myself 'straight' because it conveys a certain type of message, perhaps of superiority, with which I am not familiar. Our love for one another and our commitment to one another are great enough for us to remain united in our marriage relationship. Yet for many of our friends the road is very different.

I recall reading *Stranger at the Gate* by Mel White. It seemed to be a very reactionary book and the clear message I received from it at the time was, 'if you are gay and married to a straight partner there's no hope; get out of the relationship!' You may imagine that I was filled with some trepidation when we were to meet Mel in America. What would he say to us? The day of the planned meeting dawned and we were introduced. Before Jeremy or I could open our mouths he said, 'I'm so glad to meet you, and so relieved that you two are together.' He explained to us that one of the results of his immensely challenging book was far from what he had hoped. Many thousands were blessed, encouraged and given fresh hope and insight by his words. However, he said, there were considerable numbers of married men and women who had taken the book as a word from God to get out of their marriage, find a gay partner and divorce.

Hundreds of people had written to Mel and poured out their stories explaining their relief that they could at last believe that the door was open. They could take fresh courage and separate themselves from their marriage partners. Mel was devastated by this. He felt that he must write a personal letter to every individual who had responded in this way. He explained to every gay man and woman who had written to him in this vein that his book was never meant to be a licence for divorce. For Mel and his wife it had been right to separate and start again. For one couple it may be God's best to part; for others it will not be. There is no one rule for all.

These are some of the things I think most important for those who find themselves in a gay-straight 'mixed marriage'.

1. The world is a challenging place to be. Commitment has become a negatively loaded word. Yet the world is a far poorer place for lack of loyal relationships. Here in the West there are so many lonely people living in anonymity, isolation, hopelessness or despair, lacking significance and without any meaningful connection with another human being. The world is a better place when there are committed, faithful relationships where people can find solace, comfort, joy and courage. Everyone, gay or straight, can be an example of the kind of faithfulness that Ruth demonstrated to Naomi so long ago.

2. If a partner is unfaithful, this inevitably brings feelings of betrayal, despair and misery. It becomes an uphill journey to forgive and, if the betrayal occurs often, the road to forgiveness gets steeper and much trickier to negotiate. When betrayal occurs on a frequent basis, this seems to me to release a destructive force into any partnership which is almost impossible to assuage. Perhaps then, a word from God is needed if the partnership is to continue.

3. Honesty is important in any relationship. To face our pain and fear and to own them releases God's grace into the situation. I believe it is almost universally true that God will not cover what we are not prepared to uncover.

4. We need ongoing support to face a seemingly continuous onslaught of judgement and rejection. Some people are openly hostile to gay people and exclude them. This cannot but have a negative impact on a mixed marriage. Some people simply will not deal with the subject at all. Presumably they feel threatened or undermined, so they say, 'It doesn't affect me' and this neatly closes the subject. I can readily bring to mind examples of this. One pastor said to me, 'I don't think the subject is relevant to us as a church. We want to get on with the more important issues'. I already knew that there were at least nine gay people in that church, but they had to be submerged and were unable to be themselves because the ministers wouldn't look at the issue. Some people believe that to be gay is incompatible with Christianity and pronounce their judgment accordingly. Sometimes, also, I detect a hidden agenda in gay people which is one of judgement about our marriage — that we will never be happy, or that marriage will not survive.

So what of Jeremy and me? We are no strangers to the cost of pioneering. Before we married, I had already known what it was to face controversy and hostility. I had often come across both men and women who wouldn't speak to me as a leader simply because of my gender. I vividly recall an occasion when I had been invited to attend a leaders' conference consisting of about fifty men and one other woman. When it came to lunch time, the men scrambled to find tables where they could sit together. There were many spaces on my table but, rather than sit with me, they borrowed the chairs and sat squashed up together on other, all-male tables.

Issues around women in leadership are very similar to those faced in the gay world. We have to cope with prejudice, the judgments of others, attempts to control and domineer. Any marginalised group will face the same type of resistance to acceptance by the main group.

Jeremy, too, was aware of the price of breaking new ground. We already had a kindred spirit long before we married. For as long as our relationship has existed we have been aware of each other's perspectives. We had already developed a good friendship before our relationship took a deeper turn. Moreover, I would probably never have been able to cope with strident masculinity. Jeremy is kind and gentle, yet secure in who he is. Jeremy, I discovered, had always felt warmly towards me, years before I knew it.

I think that, for those people who have previously lived in a gay context, it must be vastly more difficult to remain committed to a heterosexual partnership. I must never say it would be impossible, but I sense that the chances of being happy in a gay-straight partnership are greatly decreased if there is a longing to be connected with someone of the same sex. Perhaps those who have this kind of feeling are absolutely gay and others who don't are less gay. Who knows? But Jeremy and I have realised over the years that there is a different dimension at work in those who have been actively gay or who have a longing for same-sex connection as opposed to others who know what it is to be attracted to members of the same gender but have not acted to a significant degree on that attraction.

Most importantly, and for whatever reason, God has put in our hearts a love for each other which surpasses all our challenges about our identity or calling, leader or not, gay or not, straight or not. We have certainly had our struggles, sometimes played out in a public arena, but like every married couple, we have had to work them through.

How arrogant we can sometimes be when, in effect, we challenge the Creator of our universe and tell him that his salvation isn't quite great enough to cover all sin and all sinners. Many times in the biblical text we are given the message that God's salvation is full and complete and encompasses all people. Some gay people find it hard to believe that they can be Christian and gay. Many more straight Christians have that difficulty. Yet how can we imagine that our God would offer a strictly limited salvation; he did not, he does not and he will not. Many times I ask God to deliver me from this or that, yet what he often wants to give me is grace in my situation and even despite my situation. So it is with gay-straight partnerships.

Prejudice is an emotional reaction, and it is my firm conviction that it can never be dealt with by argument or even biblical text. This is because it is irrational and, like many irrational fears, it must be faced. This can only occur within loving relationships where trust is developed. In a place of safety we can at last look the spectre in the face and be freed. Someone said to me recently, 'How can I be informed yet not influenced by your arguments?' What an odd question. I realised that it was an expression of fear – clever, but fearful none the less. This person wanted to convey to us that he had listened but he was not prepared to change his mind, and if that's not prejudice, I'm not Bren Marks.

We may yet face many challenges but *let us run the race with patience... reward awaits'.*

Bren Marks

Bren Marks is author of the book,

"The Turning Tide: Women in leadership in the House Church"

Originally published by Marshall Pickering, the book is now out of print. However, we do still have some copies available, from the Courage office, for £3 + £1 postage & packing (in the UK). If you are interested in obtaining a copy, please write enclosing a cheque made out to "Mrs B Marks" to:

Courage, PO Box 848, GUILDFORD, GU1 2ZY

Afterword

Dave Tomlinson

During the late 1990s I worked for a year or so as the chaplain of Mildmay Hospital in London, which treats people with HIV and AIDS. In my first week there I met a man, who I'll call Brian. He was a beautiful person, a camp Noel Coward type, probably in his early fifties. I liked him very much as I sat and talked with him, but he was deeply depressed, and it all came down to religion. He'd long since abandoned his Christian upbringing, but somehow it had never quite abandoned him. He couldn't escape the feeling that God hated him. And it was driving him crazy. I assured him that God did not hate him, and tried to offer him a different interpretation of Christianity that accepted and affirmed gay people. He thanked me for this and wept in my arms, but it didn't seem to help. He was about to go home for a short break, so before the car came to pick him up we made an arrangement to meet the following Wednesday when he returned to the hospital. However, when I arrived at work on Monday morning I was told that Brian had committed suicide in his home.

I was depressed and felt a sense of failure. At his funeral the following week, we were scattering his ashes on the roof garden when his mother screamed out in the middle of the service. She was essentially screaming at the Church. 'Why have you done this to my son?' she asked, with an agony and pain that penetrated the soul. 'Why have you persecuted him? He was a beautiful, beautiful man, why did you have to drive him to this?' I had no answer, other than to say that I believed Brian was now at peace in the bosom of the God who, despite the best efforts of many Christians to argue otherwise, loved and welcomed people like Brian.

There are as many gay people in and around the Church as any other sector of society. Many, perhaps most, feel the need to conceal their identity. Many also live with the kind of inner shame or self-hatred that Brian felt. And it is a scandal. Gay people do not choose to be gay any more than people choose their gender, or the colour of their skin, or their dominant hand. Yet a community that claims to worship the God of grace so often burdens them with guilt and shame.

Jeremy Marks' story, and the story of *Courage*, is remarkable and inspirational. As anyone who knows Jeremy understands, he is a gentle person who naturally avoids confrontation; yet, along with his wife Bren, he has fearlessly followed his convictions in the face of vitriolic opposition, personal rejection, and financial loss. Yet he has remained dedicated to the cause of supporting gay Christians and their families, and unwavering in his evangelical faith.

Courage is a vital ministry. It offers safe space — room for people to explore both their sexuality and their faith, and the inter-relationship between the two. I wish Brian could have read this book and embarked on the spiritual journey that Courage affirms and nurtures. Perhaps he would be alive today. Perhaps he would have learned to love God and love himself as a gay man.

Some people think that the words 'gay' and 'Christian' do not belong together. This book shows otherwise. May it contribute to the inevitable movement toward a more open, welcoming and inclusive church for all people.

by Dave Tomlinson
June 2008

Dave Tomlinson is vicar of St Luke's Church , Holloway, North London.

To find out more about the church and his ministry, visit www.saintlukeschurch.org.uk

For events of special interest, visit: www.breathingspace.info

Dave Tomlinson is also the author of a number of books, including:

The Post Evangelical
Running into God: Reflections for Ordinary Days
I shall not want: Spiritual Wisdom from the 23rd Psalm

Re-Enchanting Christianity *(NEW: to be available from August 2008)*

Same-sex partnerships that last

For those who do not believe gay relationships can last, and as a tribute to
the many personal friends who have come through the years of trial and
`believed God blesses same-sex partnerships, I am listing over one hundred
partnerships between people I know reasonably well, who are living
together in long-term committed relationships:

Bruce and Arief	Paul and Anthony
Dirk and Patrick	Doug and Tony
David and Allan	Craig and Marcus
Sue and Deidre	Don and David
Māris and Andis	John and Tony
Mervyn and David	Trevor and Duncan
Randolph and Rick	Debbie and Sarah
James and Feling	Andrew and Simon
Ian and Philip	Mark and Rick
Peter and Jeff	Simon and Tony
Len and Gary	Brenda and Pam
John and Mike	Nelson and Jeffrey
Lionel and James	Ian and Roger
Leon and Marc	Tony and Gavin
Jonathan and Zairul	Ojalae and David
Dan and Erik	Rachel and Sarah
Roger and Ross	Alex and David
David and Gary	Bill and James
Paul and Alvaro	Clare and Philippa
Richard and Ed	Simon and Kevin
Debbie and Carla	Murray and Lyndon
Paul and Steve	Alex and David
Chris and Roy	Mark and Daryl
Paul and Amir	Peter and Ihar
Margaret and Sarah	Howard and David
Sigrid and Sylvia	Stephen and Peter
Patrick and Ian	Philip and Steven
Louis and William	Jeffrey and Grant
Andrew and Ashley	Andy and Allan
Jason and Mark	Martin and Robert
Peter and Duncan	Bill and Ed
Amanda and Catherine	Richard and Michael

Martin and David	Margaret and Morag
Brian and Nigel	Martin and Chris
Mel and Gary	Michael and Brian
Malcolm and Brian	Michael and Marc
Mike and Andy	Ian and Norman
Huw and Alex	Andy and Norman
Gary and Mervyn	Martin and Tony
John and Julian	Patrick and Keith
Ruth and Alison	Alexis and Graham
Neil and Duncan	Andy and David
Nick and Derek	Tony and Allen
Trevor and Matthias	Tim and Steve
Lyndon and David	Stephen and Derek
Andrew and Adrian	George and Edward
Jeff and Will	John and Leo
Chris and David	Gareth and Thomas
Doug and Bruce	Andrew and Michael
Douglas and Keith	Matthew and Darren
Simon and Leslie	Andrew and Noel
Ron and Jay	David and Stephen
Richard and Ben	Peter and Colin
John and Joe	Ladonna and Pat

Notes

1 I have not specifically included transgendered folk, along with lesbian, gay and bi-sexual Christians, because although I am empathetic and supportive, their situation raises complex issues that I do not have the experience to speak on. Both gay and transgendered people suffer similar persecution and prejudice arising out of ignorance. Theologically, however, the issues do not make as straightforward a comparison as might at first appear.   For instance, paradoxically, I have met one or two conservative evangelical Christian leaders who reject homosexuality unequivocally, but have far less difficulty in accepting sex-reassignment surgery. The situation is true for some Muslims too. Iran, for instance, executes gay people, but routinely performs more reassignment operations than any other country in the world apart from Thailand, according to a recent BBC TV documentary broadcast on 25th February 2008. This raises theological questions that are beyond the scope of this book.

2 Then known as *The New Life Church*, Harrow.

3 The *Love in Action* ministry as founded by Frank Worthen, where I participated and trained, is now known as *New Hope: www.newhope123.org*

4 James Alison, San Francisco, February 2006, *Is it ethical to be Catholic?* For further articles and information about books by James Alison's, see the *Courage* website and also www.jamesalison.co.uk

5 See Stephen Green's profoundly depressing book, *The Sexual Dead-End* available from *www.christianvoice.org.uk* .

6 The *Christian Institute* website is: *www.christian.org.uk*

7 See *Mud and Stars:* Report of a working party on the impact of the hospice experience on the churches' ministry of healing. Oxford: Sobell Publications

8 Shakespeare *Hamlet* I, 3

9 Romans 2:1 James Alison gave a brilliant exposition of Romans 1, at one of our *Courage* meetings a few years ago. This is available on the *Courage* website on the *Articles* page, and also in his recent book *Undergoing God* published by DLT, under the chapter heading *But the Bible says....*

10 See Bruce Bagemihl, *Biological Exuberance*, Profile Books 1999

11 Marsha Stevens of Balm Ministries, see *www.balmministries.net*

12 See *Homosexuality: A New Christian Ethic*, by Elizabeth R Moberly, Publ. James Clarke & Co. Cambridge

13 Carol Grever, *My Husband is Gay*, The Crossing Press , p32

14 Dietrich Bonhoeffer, *Life Together*, SCM Press, 1972, pp.75-6.

15 Horrifying stories of male rape in US prisons on the Human Rights Watch website are documented on: *www.hrw.org*. See also *Violence: reflections on a national epidemic*, by James Gilligan M.D. Publ. Vintage New York.

16 *Surviving Thalidomide* Documentary directed by Benetta Adamson

17 Brian D. McLaren explores this theme in his excellent book, *A New Kind of Christian.*

18 *Special pleading*: a legal term that describes a form of spurious argumentation where a position in a dispute introduces favourable details or excludes unfavourable details by alleging a need to apply additional considerations without proper criticism of these considerations themselves. Essentially, this involves someone attempting to cite something as an exemption to a generally accepted rule, principle, etc. without justifying the exemption. (Wikipedia)

19 For a fascinating study of the meaning of *eunuch* in the Bible, see *www.well.com/user/aquarius* researched by Faris Malik.

20 See Matt Ridley's fascinating book, *Nature via Nurture.*

21 For further information about the work of Dr Ralph Blair and *Evangelicals Concerned*, see *www.ecinc.org* See also, *www.ecwr.org* for *Evangelicals Concerned, Western Region.*

22 I can highly recommend Jeffrey John's excellent book on the subject, *The Meaning in the Miracles*, published by Canterbury Press.

23 Steve Shaw, *Dancing with your Shadow*, p25.

24 Jeremy Marks, *Same-Sex Relationships and Scripture*: see Articles section at www.courage.org.uk   Also highly recommended: *Permanent, Faithful, Stable*, by Jeffrey John, Publ. Darton, Longman & Todd

25 See the *Roy Clements archive* on *www.courage.org.uk* for the full article: *Why evangelicals must think again about homosexuality.*

26 Christine Bakke and Peterson Toscano's initiative to set up the Beyond ex-gay website can be seen at: *www.beyondexgay.com*

27 *Soulforce* is a LGBT — lesbian, gay, bisexual and transgender — civil rights organisation in the USA. See *www.soulforce.org*

28 *www.soulforce.org/article/1226*

29 The full text of the former ex-gay leaders' public apology can be found at *www.beyondexgay.com/article/apology*

30 Reported in Christianity Today on 1ˢᵗ October 2000. John Paulk's story inspired Wayne Beson's book, *Anything but Straight: Exposing the Scandals and Lies Behind the Ex-Gay Myth.*

31 *Shibboleth* (Judges 12:6)—a kind of linguistic password: A way of speaking (a pronunciation, or the use of a particular expression) that identifies one as a member of an 'in' group. The purpose of a shibboleth is exclusionary as much as inclusionary: A person whose way of speaking violates a shibboleth is identified as an outsider and thereby excluded by the group. (This phenomenon is part of the 'Judge a book by its cover' tendency apparently embedded in human cognition, and the use of language to distinguish social groups). *(Words in English public website)*

32 James Alison, San Francisco, February 2006, *Is it ethical to be Catholic?* For further articles and information about books by James Alison's, see the *Courage* website and also www.jamesalison.co.uk

33 Peter Rollins, *How (Not) to Speak of God*, SPCK

34 See Dr Roy Clements' excellent exposition of Galatians 1 and Romans 14 entitled *Weaker Brothers and Damnable Heretics* at the *Roy Clements archive* on *www.courage.org.uk*

35 Richard Wurmbrand, *In God's Underground*, Hodder & Stoughton, page 102.

* * *

N.B. Courage UK is not the Catholic ministry promoting chastity founded by Father John Harvey (based in New York, with other branches worldwide). Details about that organisation, may be found at www.couragerc.org. The UK branch of CourageRC (known as EnCourage) can be found at www.encouragetrust.org.uk.